CONTENTS

About the Author

John Bowden MA, FNSEAD has been involved in art education for the past 40 years. He taught in all school phases before spending 27 years as a Senior Art Adviser in a large LEA. Currently he is part-time Lecturer in Art and Design Education at two PGCE centres, a DFES Specialist Schools assessor and a freelance art education consultant delivering INSET and offering advice on curriculum development in schools. He is also a practising artist.

He was featured in the Sainsbury schools TV programme working with pupils in the Tate Gallery, and writes the art and design 'ideas' section for weekly articles in the TES Teacher's magazine. He is also Editor of A'N'D, the NSEAD curriculum development newsletter/magazine for art and design and was Lead Writer on the NESTA Project producing guidance for teachers of talented pupils in the creative arts.

Twice he has served as Chairperson of the national Association of Advisers and Inspectors in Art and Design, and he was President of the National Society for Education in Art and Design for three years. Currently he represents the primary phase on the NSEAD Council.

INTRODUCTION

In 2003-2005 sections of this book were serialised in the NSEAD primary magazine **START**.

I have been encouraged by many requests from readers to publish this handbook now as one complete volume. The content has been extensively revised providing essential guidance for the subject leader for art and design in primary schools.

In my many years as an art and design adviser in a large LEA I worked with a number of subject leaders who welcomed support from someone like myself with specific subject expertise, who understood the difficulties in leading a minority subject and recognised the frustrations of assisting other teachers, who had little training or a limited grounding in the subject. On the many in-service training courses that I now run I continue to recognise the need for accessible support material for teachers in the field, which is practical and realistic.

In recent years external advisory support has decreased and attendance at CPD courses has become more difficult. Subject leaders in foundation subjects have increasingly felt isolated and unsupported in their role. As a subject leader you may be full of zeal to make your primary school a centre of excellence, where art is the driving force for all curriculum subjects but will probably recognise that the subject can have a low priority in comparison with the core curriculum. Your ambition is commendable but it will have been tempered with a dose of reality, particularly if you are in a smaller school where you also have responsibility for other major curriculum areas. There will be many demands on your time and limited opportunity to search for the information that is needed for you to fulfil effectively your role. This is where this handbook should prove its worth.

A plethora of books is already available about the teaching of the subject but these do not systematically focus on the specific challenges of being an art and design subject leader and can often provide a level of detail that can be intimidating. This book is essentially a primer that is intended to be accessible and cover all aspects of the role and responsibilities of a subject leader. It also considers ways of raising the status of art and design teaching in primary schools as well as offering the simple information that you may need to refer to, and provide as support material to untrained staff, on materials and processes, display and cross curricular initiatives. Each of these chapters will provide valuable information to help you to successfully establish and develop the subject in your school – to become an effective subject leader who can 'make a difference'.

John Bowden
September 2005

SECTION ONE THE EFFECTIVE SUBJECT LEADER

THE BACKGROUND OF THE SUBJECT LEADER

Chapter one

In every primary school a subject leader should be appointed to be responsible for leading art and design activities and developments. It is an important and exciting role to occupy. OFSTED, in a primary art and design Report noted that "...high standards are found where there is strong subject leadership underpinned by a commitment to the subject from the head teacher".

However, unlike secondary schools, where teachers usually only teach one subject, most primary teachers are responsible for teaching all curriculum subjects; some teachers, may have a larger portfolio of responsibilities if the school is a small institution. Inevitably some will lack the background and expertise in a particular discipline and the available time for subject leader activities is very limited. Understandably some subject leaders admit that their involvement in art and design development activities is curtailed by the demands of everyday teaching. It is indeed an important, exciting role, but also a particularly challenging one that cannot be fulfilled effectively without reasonable subject knowledge.

Developing your subject expertise
Ideally the subject leader should be a member of staff who has had some training in art and design, though you may well not term yourself as a specialist. However it is possible that you have a degree in an entirely different subject and have inherited your position despite your limited background. Unfortunately not all initial teacher education courses even offer a discrete art and design component in their training programmes, or devote a significant period of time to such activities if they do so. Some head teachers even choose to rotate subject leader responsibility roles around their staff; though this does offer additional career experience, this practice can be counter-productive if teachers are required to occupy a new role with real limitations on their expertise.

So whatever your background, you should undertake a personal audit of your knowledge and understanding to ensure that your training priorities are established and addressed. Knowing what you do not know is the first stage of personal development. Indeed, irrespective of initial training, further and regular continuing professional development (CPD) is essential if a subject leader is to maintain good subject knowledge and develop their expertise.

The National Society for Education in Art & Design (NSEAD) can provide you with contacts that can offer CPD courses, either externally or to a group in your school or an area cluster of subject leaders. Select your CPD according to your particular needs. If you have a limited art background, say less than Advanced level GCE standard, you may well prioritise practical 'hands-on' activity to learn more about basic materials and processes, but if you have an art college background then a course which centres on a higher level specialist activity or one which explores the subject leader's role in greater depth may be more appropriate. Reference to journals and websites is also important. Subscription to the NSEAD's START magazine is an essential investment, which also provides full access to the extensive NSEAD web site **www.nsead.org**. Help and guidance is always available from NSEAD to support even the most inexperienced subject leader who is determined to use their role to provide a broad primary school art and design experience for pupils. So make an early appointment to lobby the head teacher for a share in the schools CPD budget for your training. The world of art and design education is constantly changing and as the person charged with subject leadership in your school you must try to keep abreast with new developments.

THE ROLE AND RESPONSIBILITIES OF THE POST

Chapter two

Many of the additional roles and responsibilities of the subject leader are generic, though each curriculum subject presents discrete challenges related to specific subject content; for instance a practical subject such as art and design presents special problems related to organisation and management of artistic media. This chapter considers these key subject responsibilities.

Raising the profile of art and design in the school

Inevitably, in many primary schools, priority and status are usually given to the co-ordinating roles related to literacy and numeracy, as these areas are key indicators when evaluating the performance of the primary school pupil against national criteria. It will be of no surprise to read that OFSTED wrote in an annual summary report that 'The successes of primary art built up over several years are under threat on two fronts: increasing numbers of schools are allocating less time for art and design; and there is a growing tendency for art and design to be seen solely as servicing other subjects'. Thus the proactive art and design subject leader must explore ways of raising the profile of the subject within the school to ensure that it is given independence and status. This may be a challenge in the current educational climate, but in my experience many primary schools continue to recognise the unique contribution that art and design can make to the development of the primary pupil, and in these schools

I invariably meet enthusiastic subject leaders driving developments forward with determination.

Development planning

In order to do this effectively the subject leader must audit practice in the school, identifying subject strengths and areas for development, as well as recognising the limitations of the school in terms of teacher expertise and resources. As everyone teaching in the school must be involved in this audit, the next chapter will provide you with a schedule for this purpose. When the audit is completed and the responses analysed, it should indicate development needs that will have to be prioritised in order to identify a number of development areas. Development needs will vary according to the school context and everything cannot be done at once. The final outcome of this process, if structured appropriately, should result in a development plan that is the focus for change, and provide a development 'diary' to inform outside agencies, such as OFSTED or the LEA. A framework for development planning is also presented in the next chapter.

Establishing a policy and scheme of work for art and design

This is a key responsibility for the art and design subject leader. Without such documentation there cannot be a coherent and consistent whole school approach to the subject. The art and design curriculum should be broad, balanced and

address National Curriculum requirements – appropriate documentation identifies the extent of the school's ambitions.

There are three related parts to a typical set of school subject documents:

- A **policy** is a general statement of intent related to key aspects of the delivery of the subject, presenting aims and objectives, assessment strategies, strategies for differentiation according to ability, principles for inclusion, etc.

- The **scheme of work** (or curriculum plan) outlines the programme of skills, knowledge and understanding that will be taught to each year group consistently to ensure progression.

- The third, supplementary section that many subject leaders provide for staff to assist in raising standards is a **guidance document**, which offers help to those who wish to extend their knowledge about teaching skills or appreciate fully the properties of differing media.

The art and design subject leader will need to have an understanding of the essential contents of a policy, and the procedures that are necessary to ensure that an effective and usable scheme of work is established. It is helpful, if the school has no current scheme of work, to use as a template for planning a sample overall plan, which can be modified according to school needs. In England,[1] the relationship between the Qualifications and Curriculum

…the subject leader may well be required to arrange and deliver in-house training.

Authority (QCA) units of work and the school curriculum plan is also important, as an effective synthesis between the two is desirable. In order that staff 'sign up' to these important documents they need to be involved in their development through a series of staff development activities.

Establishing a whole school assessment policy

Assessment in relation to art and design in the primary school is underdeveloped, despite the introduction in England of National Curriculum levels for assessment purposes at the end of each Key Stage. This is partly because these levels are complex though it is possible to break them down into three strands to make them more user friendly. A further constraint on the introduction of assessment procedures is the belief of some teachers that art 'cannot be assessed', confusing the absolute judgements made about information centred subjects like mathematics with the criterion based moderated procedures used in the creative subjects.

The art and design subject leader needs to devise a manageable assessment system, which is understood by all staff and used consistently throughout the school to ensure that pupils know what they have to do in order to improve their performance. A portfolio of exemplar materials, mainly examples of a range of pupils' work assembled according to year groupings, indicating standards of achievement measured against National Curriculum levels should be compiled. This should be reviewed regularly and used to standardise judgements about the assessment of pupils' work.

There is a National Curriculum requirement in England to report to parents at the end of Key Stage 1 and 2 – the QCA website states that 'The National Curriculum level descriptions provide the basis for making judgements about pupils' performance at the end of Key Stages 1, 2 and 3.' (See **www.qca.org.uk**) Subject leaders should note however that the use of the National Curriculum levels to report to parents is only *mandatory* at Key Stage 3 for art and design. If you are confident that any alternative assessment procedures that are in place in your school are both comprehensive and effective then there is no requirement to use the National Curriculum levels. If however the National Curriculum levels are used for assessment purposes in the school, then in my view it would be sensible also to use them to report to parents.

You are ultimately responsible for ensuring that effective assessment procedures have been established for the subject and systematic assessment takes place. Development activities with staff are likely to be needed to reduce confusion make assessment work effectively.

Identifying and arranging staff development and training

An outcome of your whole school audit may well be that some staff need assistance and guidance teaching the subject. Each member of staff has a right to appropriate training but in the primary school it may well be that it is not possible to offer individual subject training outside the institution due to cost and time constraints. Therefore the subject leader, having identified particular needs, may well be required to arrange and deliver 'in house' in-service training, this might be to develop skills (e.g. three-dimensional work) or involve staff in curriculum planning activities. Small schools often combine to share training activities and their common expertise.

Monitoring performance

Some time should be devoted to monitoring staff performance and the delivery of the subject throughout the school in terms of both curriculum coverage and standards. As an OFSTED inspector I recognise that opportunities for this to take place are limited, due to the constraints I described in the introduction. 'The one area where practice continues to remain relatively underdeveloped – despite its importance – is the monitoring of teaching in art and design' states an OFSTED summary report. To be completely effective monitoring should involve lesson observation and the subject leader will have to ensure that this is done in a non-threatening manner, and that an observation schedule is agreed in advance. There may be a generic lesson observation schedule in use in the school but this might have to be supplemented by subject specific teaching requirements, recognising that art and design is often concerned with practical work.

Obviously there are other strategies for monitoring the way in which the subject is being delivered in the school. The subject leader should regularly take the opportunity to view pupils' work that is on display in classes, and occasionally examine staff planning and assessment sheets, to ensure that the subject is being delivered consistently and recorded and assessed effectively. Much can be learnt by such informal monitoring procedures although, ideally, active classroom observation and support also should be taking place.

What is most important, particularly in larger schools, is to gain an overview of what is happening in all classrooms. Having some excellent but overall variable practice

in your school is an unsatisfactory situation and you need to have a clear picture of this in order to address the problem.

Managing resources

There may be a limited budget for the subject, together with opportunities for some capital outlay. Each year the subject leader will have the responsibility for either spending this budget and/or advising other staff on the most appropriate materials and equipment to purchase. Significant resource expenditure should be driven by the long-term needs identified in the development plan rather than individual short-term staff demands.

Systems for delivery and distribution of these resources are also the responsibility of the coordinator, for some resources will be kept centrally and shared (e.g. critical studies resources), whilst others will be held in individual classrooms

(e.g. basic art materials). It is important to ensure that systems are consistent and that materials and resources are stored and distributed efficiently, without waste.

You may also be responsible for firing a kiln, but the wise subject leader should ensure that all teachers share the responsibility for this task. You should not allow yourself to become the art technician.

Innovative curriculum initiatives

Effective co-ordination of the subject involves innovation as well as organisation. Some of the most exciting art work I see is produced by using 'artists in schools' effectively, or in 'art weeks' when the regular curriculum is suspended allowing concentration for a longer period on one subject. Such initiatives are usually the result of imaginative thinking by the art and design subject leader.

2

Illustrations 1-4 inclusive: Staff INSET workshop activities

Managing transition from Key Stage 2 to Key Stage 3

Secondary art and design teachers often comment that they have to start again with pupils they receive in Year 7 because of variations in experience, given that the group comprises pupils from differing primary schools, some of which have limited provision in art and design. What you will want to avoid is for your pupils to be given tasks that repeat what they have already done. The first proactive task is to make contact with the appropriate heads of department to share your carefully developed curriculum plan with them and arrange a visit to the secondary schools.

Then ascertain from your school's General Adviser/Inspector if the primary feeder schools meet as a 'cluster' and ask if you can talk to the art and design subject leaders at some point to establish a corporate approach to both assessment and the knowledge and skills that will be covered in all the feeder primary schools; this is increasingly happening when primary schools are feeding into a specialist art college. Invite the secondary art teachers to the meeting also, though be wary of letting them tell you what you should be doing – a secondary practitioner may not necessarily understand your primary art approach or the early year's context. They should be co-operative if you take this initiative, for once they are confident that pupils who transfer at the end of Key Stage 2 have had a more consistent understanding of the subject and possess some common basic skills, there will be no reason to treat every Year 7 pupil as a beginner.

Summary

The role of the art and design subject leader is indeed challenging and this list of responsibilities may seem daunting, but it does of course represent the ideal, which may not be deliverable in every school. Different contexts provide constraints, as well as opportunities. However without active and confident leadership the subject is unlikely to flourish; your start in auditing practice, consulting staff and producing a long-term development plan and a strategy to implement it are presented in the next two chapters.

[1] There is probably more central control of the curriculum in England than the rest of the United Kingdom. While this book sometimes makes specific reference to English institutions such as OFSTED and QCA, there are often organisations with similar roles elsewhere and some material such as the QCA Schemes of Work may be of interest – at least for reference – wider afield.

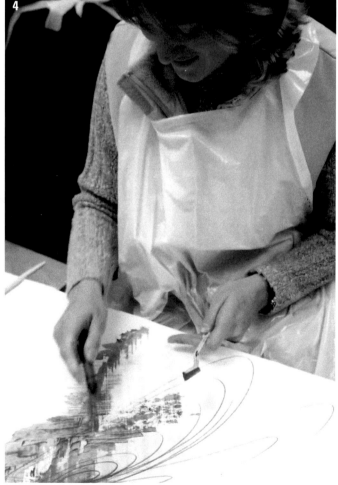

AUDITING PRACTICE AND PRIORITISING DEVELOPMENT AREAS

Chapter three

Having read chapter two it may be that you are now overwhelmed by the range of possible activities you could engage in as part of your role as subject leader. Where should you start?

You should commence your responsibilities by auditing practice and establishing a development plan. Development planning has become a familiar feature of activity in all primary schools as instituting change is now recognised as essential if any subject is to develop. An inspector will expect to see a development plan which has taken into account weaknesses that have been identified (if any) from the last inspection report. However irrespective of this external perspective the proactive subject leader will want to move practice forward by making changes that have been agreed through active consultation and are therefore supported by all staff. The development plan states your ambition for change and everyone will know what you want them to focus on systematically in order to achieve your goals.

The development plan
Your development plan will have to prioritise issues, as there are likely to be more areas for development than can be realistically achieved in the generally accepted three year planning cycle. Usually development plans are presented as a table and a column for each of the following areas will be needed. For each stated *development objective* the development plan should explain *why that area has been identified* for development activity, outline *the*

strategy that will achieve it, state *who will be responsible for monitoring progress, what the resource implications are* (if any), *when the objective will be achieved and finally how its success will be measured.*

Prioritising objectives
Deciding what your development objectives are is more difficult and you would be unwise to do this without consulting others. To decide independently and arbitrarily what is going to be targeted in a development plan will achieve little – without whole staff support development objectives cannot be attained. Therefore if all staff are to have 'ownership' of the development process the strategy that has been used to identify prioritised objectives needs to be transparent. Every member of staff needs to be involved and consulted. You could be even more radical and ask some pupils what they would like to change in their art education.

Simply asking staff in a staff meeting what changes they feel are necessary will not be constructive. Some staff may have particular and idiosyncratic views and others may be just indifferent. Your strategy should be two-fold. First you should systematically audit what is, and just as importantly what is not, taking place and, second, consult staff using a formal questionnaire to reinforce your informal information gathering.

The audit
The informal starting point is to spend time discreetly observing what is going on without making uninvited observations and

complete the checklist that follows which then can be shared with all staff. I have found this personal checklist very helpful in my in-service work because it covers all the key areas that need to be audited. You will see that the survey comprises a series of questions, each of which requires a Yes/No response. It may be that you cannot make such an absolute judgement – the 'yes-but' case will mean that you are starting to delve deeper into your particular schools situation. As a starting point this checklist can be enlightening because, in theory, any question that has been given a negative response by the subject leader is a potential area for development. However even if you disagree with the outcomes, the analysis will have commenced. Remember this survey is based on my personal vision about best practice in primary art and design education that not everyone will agree with. Even if you disagree with my perspective the document will have served another important purpose in that it will have helped define your personal philosophy.

If you have a negative response to one or more questions, from your perspective there may be very clear and valid reasons for this. For instance, I believe that there should be a balanced programme of two-dimensional and three-dimensional work. Your school may have acknowledged this but nevertheless consciously prioritised one particular area, perhaps to capitalise on staff strengths or ensure adequate depth of experience for pupils. (See the depth versus breadth issue considered in

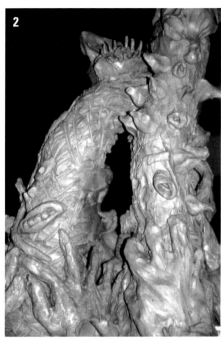

the chapter on curriculum planning.) If this is the case, even with a 'No' response you will obviously choose not to select this as a development area. Equally you may have already considered and rejected an identified development area highlighted by the honest completion of this checklist, because of significant and insurmountable constraints. For instance you may recognise the need for large-scale work but classroom space could make this ambition unrealistic. Thus, by using the checklist analytically and flexibly as a basis for discussion, your individual school art and design development priorities can be established corporately.

Remember that reaching a decision about prioritised development areas must draw on all information you have gathered as well as your audit. Look at work on classroom walls and in folders, talk with staff and pupils who are eager to show you their work, and see how effectively materials are organised and presented. Formal lesson observation will provide more evidence. All this information should be taken into account before decisions are made, and it is important to remember that your finalised development plan must be realistic and be achievable in the timescale. In addition the staff questionnaire will provide a different perspective. Some help with establishing a strategy for change is provided in the next chapter.

But first your starting point for change...

Complete this CHECKLIST!

1. Management of the subject

Does the subject leader have an art and design training, at least to equivalent of GCE Advanced level?

Has the subject leader attended at least one art and design CPD course recently?

Does the subject leader have only art and design within their management brief in the school?

Is the subject leader allocated some specific non-contact time for development activity in the subject?

Does the subject leader regularly monitor, through lesson observation, the delivery of the subject in classrooms throughout the school?

Has the subject been identified as a development area in the school in the last five years?

Has the subject leader addressed staff about key issues in the subject for the purpose of development at either a staff meeting or on a training day (i.e. in the last three years)?

Does the school have a written art and design policy?

Does the art and design policy cover all of the key areas identified in the earlier chapter on policy content?

Does the school have an overall plan/ scheme of work for the subject that identifies skills, knowledge and understanding that is progressively developed across the key stages?

Have the QCA units of work been considered and, where deemed appropriate, incorporated into the content of the overall scheme of work?

Do all members of staff follow the scheme of work?

Does the school have a programme of critical studies activities which ensures that artists and designers of both genders, from a range of cultures are introduced to pupils systematically?

Is there a development plan for art and design, which has responded to the findings of the last inspection report?

2. Curriculum provision and balance

Do all pupils in each year group, every year:

- Engage in observation recording and recall activities?
- Work from imaginative/fantasy sources?
- Explore the visual elements on a systematic basis?
- Learn new processes and explore new media?
- Draw, paint, stick, print, model and construct?
- Engage in practical critical studies activities that are not based solely on copying works of art and design?

…draw on all information for your audit – look at work on classroom walls and in folders, talk with staff and pupils who are eager to show you their work, and see how effectively materials are organised and presented.

- Engage in discussion and learn about key artists, craftpersons, designers from differing periods and cultures?
- Work in three dimensions for at least 25 percent of their allocated art time?
- Work on a variety of scales?
- Keep a sketchbook (older pupils only)?

3. Teaching style
Across the school do pupils both return to finish their work after a period as well as completing it in one lesson?

In all classes are pupils taught art and design as a specific focused subject activity, as well as engaging in art and design arising from topic activities?

Are all pupils given some direct instruction in the subject?

Are pupils encouraged to explore media freely to discover its properties?

Do pupils work on art and design tasks;
a. Individually?
b. In a group?
c. As a whole class?

(In my view effective art and design teaching should utilise a full range of these teaching styles as appropriate.)

4. Provision and resources

Does your school have adequate consumable resources to engage in all of the processes listed earlier?

Is capitation allocated each year for the purchase of consumable resources?

Is capitation allocated each year in addition for development work in the subject?

Are there tools for three-dimensional work available in each classroom, or accessible on request?

Is there a sink and a suitable 'wet area' in each room?

Is there adequate space in each room for work on a variety of scales and in different media?

Is there a set of critical studies resources of adequate scale for whole class discussion that can be circulated around classes as needed?

Does the school have a digital camera that can be used for art and design activities and appropriate computer programs to create and manipulate imagery, with computer access whenever required?

5. Allocation of curriculum time
Across the school is at least one hour a week allocated specifically for art and design activities?

Has additional 'enrichment' time been specifically allocated for the subject e.g. an art week or an artist in school?

6. Assessment procedures
Does the school use National Curriculum levels, at the end of Key Stage 1 and 2 for the purpose of reporting to parents?

Does the school use National Curriculum levels, modified as necessary, as a corporate assessment system?

If the answer to the previous question is 'No', or if your school is not in England, are there alternative assessment arrangements and practices in the school that are deemed adequate?

Is there a portfolio with a range of work of agreed standard available to assist staff in making judgements and moderate standards?

Do members of staff, on receiving pupils from a previous year group/teacher, have a clear idea of each pupil's ability in the subject?

Is pupils' work transferred from one class to another as they progress through the school?

Are certain activities repeated as pupils progress through the school in order to identify their progress in the subject?

Do pupils evaluate their personal work and that of other pupils on a regular basis?

7. Finally
Are there some questions you could not answer?

(It is arguable that an informed subject leader should be able to answer all these questions if you are being given proper opportunity to function efficiently; for instance if you cannot confidently state what is taking place in all classrooms you certainly have your first development issue.)

Illustrations 1-9 inclusive: The subject leader should
audit breadth of media and processes, the range of
curriculum content, consider whether individual, whole
class and group teaching is utilised and assess the quality
of the display and stimulus.

ESTABLISHING A STRATEGY FOR LASTING CHANGE

Chapter four

Although I have already advocated that the subject leader should lead by example, by being a shining beacon of personal good practice, some staff may not recognise your endeavours, or be influenced by them. The ultimate test of a subject leader's effectiveness is the extent to which they are able to influence practice in art and design and institute lasting change throughout the school, ensuring a consistent experience for every pupil. This can be a challenge.

Many subject leaders tell me they have inherited a role in a school where everything needs to be changed; their discreetly conducted audit has identified numerous examples of bad practice in art and design teaching, a lack of expertise amongst the staff, inconsistency in application of policies and low standards throughout, with indifference or even resistance to change. But it is still possible to make a difference, even in such a situation as this, if the subject leader is tactfully proactive.

The proactive subject leader

You must initially get as many people on your side as is possible. A long talk with the head teacher is your starting point, in which you will present your development plan that arises from your completed and thorough audit. Remember though that head teachers in primary schools are, more than ever before, subject to the external pressures of the national agenda. Scores in SATs, particularly in literacy and numeracy may inevitably be their priority,

rather than developing the foundation subjects in general and your passion for art and design in particular. Some head teachers may wish to offer a broad and balanced curriculum, but I find that art and design remains a relatively unimportant subject in the majority of primary schools. So, unless the head teacher has already guaranteed the necessary support from the leadership team in the pursuit of change, charging into the school office to demand immediate and radical remedial action may not be the best tactic. Trying to change everything at once may be unrealistic and may gain you a reputation as an extremist – not always the best position from which to exert influence. The wise subject leader in a conservative environment will have sensible ambitions, recognising that their powers for action may be limited but their capacity to influence is unbounded. A tactfully presented prioritised long-term strategy is more likely to achieve permanent change that really increases the impact of art and design in the school. Accompanying this should be a request for an art budget, however small, to assist the developments you wish to encourage.

The subject leader should capitalise on all opportunities to proselytise their views about the importance of art and design and the contents of the development plan. These may be formal, as in offering to address the staff at a staff meeting about the development plan, or informal, as when one is asked in the staff room about how to link a general topic from another subject with art and design. Every opportunity

should be taken to show enthusiasm and willingness to help other staff, avoiding the use of specialist terms and jargon. Always be readily available to give advice and guidance, referring staff regularly to that part of your scheme of work which offers guidance on materials and processes – the chapters in this book on materials and processes can be used for this purpose. A folder containing past copies of START magazine, carefully cross-referenced so that articles on particular processes or themes can be quickly accessed, will supplement this documentation, and there should also be a comprehensive collection of examples of pupils work available for scrutiny which demonstrate appropriate pupil achievement against National Curriculum levels, possibly recorded on a CD. Holding some key resources such as reproductions for critical studies or specialist equipment will provide opportunities to influence their use through casual discussion as they are distributed.

Establishing a policy, scheme of work and manageable assessment procedures are vital. Although in doing this it is essential to involve all staff incorporating their ideas, pet projects and favoured artists, it should not be at the expense of abandoning your key principles that underpin the subject. Imposing a policy without consultation will ensure that some will subvert it surreptitiously or simply ignore it.

Consulting staff using a questionnaire

The previously described audit is essentially for the subject leader's use, working in conjunction with the head teacher. It is the tool that will identify all key issues for the subject but it is not intended for whole staff use. It is equally important to research what everybody in the school personally thinks about the subject, to gain a realistic picture of individual staff priorities, and their varying artistic knowledge and abilities. So instead of the audit consider using the questionnaire, which is less complicated and does not use specialist terms. It will also act as a curriculum development document as it touches on many aspects of best practice. Individual reflection and open-ended responses are invited. It is a vehicle for teachers to communicate with the subject leader personally and privately, or even if they wish, anonymously. The answers received may be unexpected and sometimes negative, but at least the questionnaire will also identify those members' of staff who are positive about art and design, even if they feel they lack the expertise to move the subject forward. These are the allies who will be your important supporters in subject initiatives in the future. A group of enthusiasts can achieve much more than any individual.

The responses to the questionnaire may reveal that some teachers do not devote a specific period of time to focused art and design teaching or, at worst, merely using the subject as an opportunity to occupy and entertain. There is a limit to the way that a subject leader can change how the subject is delivered in other parts of the school without the cooperation of the head teacher, but there are some initiatives that will ensure that at least some teaching will be centred on art and design, rather than just arising from topic work. Why not suggest that there is an 'art afternoon' once a month, or an 'art week' once a year, during which all the school activities concentrate on an aspect of art and design related to particular chosen theme? Your opportunity to influence what goes on when this takes place will increase if those colleagues identified from the questionnaire as 'friends of the subject' are involved in planning and delivering the events. Why not contact a local college to ask if a team of teacher trainees could be involved in this activity or even sixth formers from a local school who study art? Their involvement and enthusiasm will certainly be a catalyst for success.

The questionnaire obliquely approaches the delicate issue of direct observation of classes by the subject leader – because teachers most in need of help in a practical subject such as art and design are probably those who are most likely to be intimidated by the process of direct observation. Giving colleagues the option of having the subject leader work alongside them, or even teaching their class whilst they watch, is more tactful than just telling them that you will first observe and then inform them how the lesson could be improved. Tact is the watchword.

The 'user friendly' survey also asks for a response on CPD needs. It may be that staff responses are different from those needs identified as a result of your completion of the more complex audit. Inexperienced staff sometimes are looking for CPD in art and design that provides just 'quick tips' for lesson activities, rather than the in depth examination of art and design education issues that you feel is needed. However CPD must accommodate everyone's perceived needs if it is to have an impact. When it is the turn of art and design for a training session, try to make the experience memorable, entertaining and non-threatening. In my CPD work I find that teachers who lack confidence will still enjoy examining the many examples of pupil's work that I have collected, some of which are used to illustrate this handbook. Practical activities are most successful if they are executed in groups and involve problem solving with materials, particularly in three-dimensions, or processes that can be demonstrated and then tried out. It may then be possible to move into areas that the novice finds more intimidating such as observational drawing. My test of the success of CPD activities is whether I leave the group with a sense of satisfaction and a positive desire for more, rather than exposing individual course member's inadequacies.

Suggestions for staff development activities are provide at the end of several following chapters. But now the next stage – distribute the questionnaire.

STAFF QUESTIONNAIRE

Dear member of staff

As the art and design subject leader I want to move the subject forward in the school but cannot do this without your co-operation and support. I am interested therefore in what you feel about the subject, what you perceive as your needs and limitations, and how I might assist you in moving forward. Could you please give me some of your time to complete this questionnaire, which can be returned to me in confidence (without your name if you wish) in order to assist me in my role? This questionnaire will give me a better understanding of practice across the school and enable me to establish a development plan that accommodates the needs of the majority of staff.

Please be as honest as possible and do not be afraid to state your limitations and concerns!

Sincerely

A N Other

1. How important do you think that art and design is within the primary curriculum?

Unimportant <1 2 3 4 5> Important

2. Please rate your ability to teach the following on a five-point scale, where 1 indicates very limited ability and 5 represents a clear confidence in teaching the content

Drawing
1 2 3 4 5

Painting
1 2 3 4 5

Print making
1 2 3 4 5

Clay work
1 2 3 4 5

Other three-dimensional activities
1 2 3 4 5

Critical studies and the history of art and design
1 2 3 4 5

Observational work
1 2 3 4 5

The visual elements of art and design
1 2 3 4 5

3. Is there any other aspect of the subject that you feel you would like support in teaching?

4. Which of the following do you do regularly with your pupils?

Drawing / Painting / Printing / Modelling / Constructing

Designing and pattern-making

Critical studies activities

Additional art activities that are not included in the above?

5. When you teach art do you:

a. Discuss the activity and identify the objectives of the lesson with pupils before you start?

Usually / sometimes / rarely

b. Demonstrate techniques with materials?

Usually / sometimes / rarely

c. Intervene if you see that pupils are having problems with the activity?

Usually / sometimes / rarely

d. Address the class collectively as well as individually during the lesson?

Usually / sometimes / rarely

e. Draw together the threads at the end of the lesson and point out aspects of particularly successful work?

Usually / sometimes / rarely

6. Who is mainly involved in the teaching of art and design in your class?

Yourself/the learning support assistant/ a parent/other (please specify)

7. Approximately how much time do you devote to teaching art and design as a separate subject each week?

8. Approximately how much additional art and design activity arises from other aspects of the curriculum?

9. Do you feel confident in your ability to assess the art and design work of pupils?

Yes / no

10. Do any of the following restrict your teaching of the subject?

Lack of personal expertise or knowledge / lack of available materials / lack of equipment / a lack of space / the demands of literacy and numeracy (Highlight as many as are appropriate)

Please amplify if you wish:

11. Do you find the school curriculum documentation for art and design helpful?

Yes / No

If no how could it be changed to make it a more useful document?

12. Are there any changes that could be instituted within the school that would make it easier for you to teach art and design?

Yes / No

Please describe these briefly:

13. Having now taken a little time to reflect on your practice in art and design, would targeted in-service training be of help to you and would you be willing to attend?

Yes / No

Please identify the area/activity you would want such training to concentrate upon:

14. In the non-contact time the art and design subject leader is given to offer support to others, which of the following would be helpful to you?

a. The art and design subject leader teaching your class or group?

Yes / No

b. A team teaching lesson in which the art and design subject leader worked with you?

Yes / No

c. The art and design subject leader observing your lesson and offering a view on your performance afterwards?

Yes / No

15. Are there any other areas of concern that have not identified in this questionnaire?

Please elaborate:

Thank you for completing this questionnaire. It will be used to help shape policy and identify future training needs.

After analysing the outcomes

My final recommendation to you as the wise subject leader is to take a long term view of development. Whatever your best efforts, there may well be those who continue to regard the benefits of art and design education with some scepticism. But this is inevitable and you should not be discouraged but rather must take a longer perspective. As more staff adopt the practices you advocate the more likely it is that the resistant minority will begin also to take notice and the quality of all pupils' creative experiences will be further enhanced.

The future of art and design education in primary schools is in your hands.

DEVELOPING A POLICY AND CURRICULUM PLAN

Chapter five

So, you have gained a picture of practice and the views of staff will have informed your development plan. It is now likely that you need to review your paperwork as a result. After all, although there are few primary schools that could not produce their example of a basic art and design policy, as a consequence of increasing awareness of the connection between effective planning and raising standards, rather more do still lack an effective, progressive scheme of work.

Although it is unlikely that your school does not have any art and design documentation, it is certainly possible that it is need of revision. This may be the result of comments from an inspector or adviser, or in response to new national initiatives and developments, or simply as part of the regular cycle of curriculum development. This chapter will now outline key requirements for this documentation, so that you can compare what is currently in place in your school with an ideal model, and consider the dilemmas facing you as subject leader when you are required to produce documentation that will enhance the process of change.

A structure for the documentation
Art and design documentation is most easily considered in three categories;

The first is the **policy** statement divided into key sections giving brief statements on aims, policy for assessment, equal opportunities, etc; the second is the **curriculum plan** (sometimes called a

scheme of work) which outlines what will be taught to pupils, and the third section, (which is not essential) comprises the **appendix**. The appendix may include supplementary guidance to staff on areas as diverse as agreed assessment procedures, the properties of specific media, to instructions on firing the kiln or display – effectively a staff art and design handbook. If the appendix offers accessible and comprehensive guidance to all staff it may ease the burden created by repeated requests for information from you, the hard-pressed subject leader.

The policy content in detail

General advice
The policy is of course the easy part, and following the outline below will probably give you a picture of practice in your school, though it must be tailored according to individual needs. This is because a policy is simple to write but, as we all know, more difficult to implement. It is essential that it accurately reflects the reality of the school's art and design practice rather than present an idealised picture. Eventually someone will measure the policy statements against actual practice and so rhetorical statements should be avoided.

Each policy statement in the policy document should be brief; if it is necessary to provide detailed information about procedures and practice mentioned in the policy this should be provided in the appendix. Nor should the art and design policy merely repeat generic statements

that are available in other general school policy documents, but should focus specifically on the art and design subject dimension.

Sections of a Policy
The document should include brief statements on the following areas:

- The rationale fronting the policy is the mission statement that underpins the school's philosophy for the subject, and may be derived from a key document on art and design education such as the National Curriculum or quote a key point from a major art educator that encompasses the importance of art and design in the primary school.

- The aims and objectives for the subject may vary according to the philosophy of the school but are likely to include: the development of visual awareness and visual literacy in pupils; the opportunity for pupils to use art to record inner feelings and express their creative imagination; the development of pupils' understanding of the visual elements of art and design; the development of pupils' critical abilities and understanding of their own and others' cultural heritages and, obviously, the opportunity to use artistic media to acquire skills and develop techniques.

- It should also include a statement on the organisation and management of the subject. Will it simply be organised by teaching through topic work or will there also be some separate subject

There is no single accepted structure for a curriculum plan but I have found that dividing the curriculum into the discrete categories of drawing, painting, printing, modeling and constructing, together with a section on the visual elements is helpful.

teaching? Without this it is unlikely to cover comprehensively the skills knowledge and understanding that are necessary.

- Incorporated in this section might be a statement about the teaching style that will be adopted generally for the subject. It is now recognised that a range of different teaching styles, including those involving direct whole class instruction, are necessary if effective 'focused' art and design teaching is to take place. The subject will be obviously be managed by you, the subject leader.

- Your role as subject leader may be outlined here, although if there is already a clear job description provided in other whole school documentation, offering a generic statement that covers the responsibilities of all subject leaders it need not be repeated.

- Your policy might also include the policy on differentiation for art and design, which though it is likely to be achieved largely by outcome, is increasingly being focused on specific differentiated tasks targeted at both the more able, or those pupils who might be disadvantaged by the verbal dimension of critical studies for instance.

- Connected to this will be the policy on equal opportunities, a key point being the importance of ensuring that stereotyping is avoided in relation to the gender of the artist, and that multicultural diversity is celebrated.

- The policy for organising materials and equipment should be stated. Usually some key resources will be held centrally and others distributed around the school (with details supplied in the appendix).

- There may well be a separate policy statement on assessment to supplement the whole school policy on assessment. In England, for example, this will focus on the requirement to assess pupils' work using the National Curriculum levels at the end of Key Stages 1 and 2, reporting to parents using National Curriculum statements (these can be presented in the appendix if required) and the need to ensure that consistency in teacher assessment for the subject is maintained through portfolio moderation procedures.

- In view of the importance of information and communication technology (ICT), a discrete policy in relation to art and design could be presented, stating its importance as a tool for learning in the subject, and the need to ensure its immediate availability for pupils engaged in visual enquiry.

- Finally include a statement asserting the value of display and presentation.

The curriculum plan

Why is this needed?
The second section of the documentation should be the curriculum plan. It is now generally recognised that there is more to art and design teaching than simply providing the opportunity to explore materials, important though this is. All subject teaching involves progressive planning with clearly identified learning objectives. To be effective this document should summarise the programme of activities for art and design that will meet the stated objectives for the subject. Some English schools have adopted the National Curriculum scheme of work published by the QCA as their overall programme. However, many schools now provide a network of progressive skills, knowledge and understanding that runs alongside these units to ensure progression and consistency. If the school already has a curriculum plan/scheme it should not automatically be replaced with the QCA units – their use is not mandatory and the units can be adapted according to need.

A structure for the plan
There is no single accepted structure for a curriculum plan, but I have found that dividing the art and design curriculum into discrete categories, such as the processes of drawing, painting, printmaking, modelling

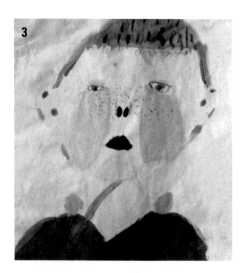

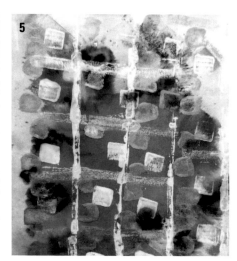

and constructing, and separating out the visual element strands is helpful. Thus:

Processes	Visual elements
Drawing	Line
Painting	Tone
Printing	Texture
Modelling	Colour
Constructing	Pattern
	Shape
	Three-dimensional form

You should identify the skills and knowledge you wish pupils to acquire in each year group, listing the learning objectives for drawing, painting, printing, modelling and constructing, with a separate though interactive plan for the visual elements of line, tone, texture, colour, pattern and shape, and three-dimensional form. Introducing pupils to differing artists, designers and craftpersons, whose work centres on a particular process or aspect of the elements in the plan, is a useful strategy to ensure that critical studies work is integrated systematically, and has clear learning objectives. In order to avoid needless repetition of a narrow range of styles of art or artists, it is necessary to provide a 'map' across year groups ensuring that there is an appropriate and balanced range of genre (e.g. landscape, portrait, still life, abstract, etc). This should include artists of both genders, work from a range of different periods and from a wide range of cultural sources.

An art curriculum plan is essentially a detailed account of the activities that will take place in each year and the skills and knowledge that will be acquired. Staff should have the flexibility to deliver this programme of artistic learning through any chosen subject matter and whatever lesson topic they wish, through both subject-centred teaching and cross-curricular activities, as long as they are addressing the learning objectives in the curriculum plan.

Breadth, balance, continuity and progression

The art and design curriculum content should be broad and balanced, and the programme that you plan should show evidence of continuity and progression. It is not simply a list of themes and topics. The range of experiences should be wide but this can create a dilemma for the curriculum planner. It might seem a simple process to identify the constituents of a broad course: pupils should be given opportunities to engage in observational work and record these observations, explore sources for imaginative work and personal expression, develop their art vocabulary and engage in activities in which they evaluate their own and others' artistic endeavours so developing their critical abilities and cultural knowledge. In doing this they are likely to engage in the processes of drawing, painting, printing, collage, modelling, constructing and using the essential tool of ICT as indicated above. However many of these activities are interactive and can therefore be covered simultaneously. For instance in doing an observational drawing pupils will learn about the properties of hard and soft pencils and be exploring the visual elements of line and tone. You will need to indicate when these aspects are important enough to be addressed discretely, and when they can be incorporated into one activity.

If it is decided that pupils are to experience all aspects of this comprehensive programme every year there is a danger of superficiality unless considerable time is provided for the subject which, to be realistic, is unlikely. Thus choices need to be made; some areas of activity will need to be prioritised, whilst retaining a balanced experience. This dilemma is often called the 'breadth versus depth' debate.

The most challenging aspect of curriculum planning is to identify sequential activities in art and design. Some subjects have clear linear progression, as in mathematics where one would hardly teach division before subtraction for instance, but in art and design it is less clearly defined where activities are revisited and reinforced in a flexible manner as a 'spiral curriculum'. However a progressive programme of activities can be established in relation to materials and processes, and the use of tools and some artistic concepts.

Some simple examples follow

Progression in relation to materials and media, and related tools is easiest to establish because most primary teachers recognise that some artistic media are simpler to use than others. Powder paint is likely to be used in all years to encourage colour mixing from a dry medium, but exploiting the properties and subtlety of watercolour is more likely to be focused on older primary pupils, and although pupils of all ages would use pencils, the subtle differences that can be gained by using pencils of a range of different hardness, from 6B to 2H might again be most appropriately introduced to older pupils. Therefore, although the majority of media and tools can be used by pupils at any time, the curriculum planner must decide at what stage pupils can most effectively exploit their potential.

Some processes are also more complicated than others. For instance potato printing and printing from junk are likely to be early

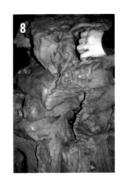

Illustrations

1-9: The model illustrated
1: Exploring shape and pattern in the visual elements
2: Drawing activity
3: Painting
4-5: Printing
6: Painting
7-8: Modelling
9: Constructing

years' activities but screen-printing or lino printing deemed more appropriate as the pupils' confidence increases. However there is no obvious progression in subject matter. Adventurous teachers now introduce quite complex issues and themes to young pupils with considerable impact; however there will need to be agreement amongst the staff in a large school to ensure that art topics are not repeated.

It may be that you disagree with my examples of progression – in this case you are probably on the way to developing your individualised curriculum, because there are no absolute rules in this debate. Unless you are the only teacher in the school involved in art and design activity a curriculum plan is essential to avoid overlap and repetition, and provide visible evidence of progress by the end of the course. Your curriculum plan will have to take account of National Curriculum requirements, of course, but the programmes of study are very broad. There are also a number of published schemes of work available that can be purchased by the subject leader. Though these plans may provide a useful model for development they should be adapted according to the individual school's need, rather than adopted in their entirety without modification. What can and will be taught varies according to school context.

The appendix
When your curriculum plan is finally produced there will inevitably be some staff who feel that their subject knowledge is too limited to teach some of its aspects effectively. In the appendix you can provide some related guidance on materials and processes to assist them. Later chapters of this book offer a basic compendium of information that

you could incorporate for this purpose. There may also be information you wish to include about available shared resources, perhaps the systems established for using the kiln or agreed guidelines for some conformity of display, etc. This third section may become quite bulky, therefore it is important to clearly separate this possibly weighty guidance section from the two previous sections to avoid confusion.

Staff Development Activity

Developing a Curriculum Plan – a whole school strategy
Curriculum development involves change in accepted working practices and you could encounter resistance from colleagues who have an established pattern of work. When you develop a curriculum plan it is important to build on existing good school practice and ensure 'ownership' by involving all staff in its development. Therefore in my work on curriculum planning with groups of teachers, I always commence with an 'audit'. I ask all staff to write down what activities pupils have experienced in art and design, and to note the medium used, the skills learnt, the visual elements that have been focused upon and aspects of art history or critical studies that have been addressed. This will be a retrospective record over a period of some months and may require reference to weekly planning.

Staff activity suggestion
In order to ensure that the aims of the policy accurately reflect practice in the school, you can ask all staff this simple question in a development meeting: 'What do we wish to achieve through the delivery of art and design in our school?' The debate will commence!

An audit sheet can be used for this task listing the medium/process, visual elements and critical studies references, if any, and providing a box to note the details of each one. The review should consider a complete year of art activities to ensure that it is representative. It is useful to ask colleagues to identify both what pupils did and the specific learning objectives for the activity.

After everyone has completed this audit you can incorporate all the responses onto one master copy for collective scrutiny. If the same media/processes, concepts, elements or artistic styles and genres have been focused on in differing year groups, this repetition will be evident. Ascertain the reason for this. Do activities differ in level or challenge, are they revisited for reinforcement or are they simply being repeated at an individual's whim, thus consuming valuable curriculum time? A staff meeting is the best place to analyse this in order to reach some conclusions about necessary changes and developments to the existing scheme of work.

THE CREATIVE CLIMATE

Chapter six

An aspect of your policy may feature display and presentation but this is only one dimension of a broader issue which if addressed will be a significant step towards your goal of raising the status of the subject in your school. Some primary inspector colleagues of past acquaintance used to claim that they could 'smell a good school'. They were not referring to a hygiene issue in this light-hearted statement, but to the fact that they felt it possible to infer from a number of different signals during a tour of a primary school the priority that had been given to the provision of a creative educational experience for pupils. Thus a display policy should not be seen in isolation, but rather as one dimension of a broader concern for the overall quality of the schools' visual environment.

Most primary school management teams are aware of the importance of making a favourable and immediate impact on everyone who visits, whether they are my inspector colleagues or others, including the parents. As they will recognise that first impressions are largely gained from visual signals and that these exert considerable influence on subsequent perceptions of visitors, they will want to support your initiative in establishing a creative climate.

Taking a new perspective
Your first step as subject leader is to review the overall visual impact of the school environment. To do this try to gain a fresh perspective by going outside the school and re-entering, adopting the role of a perhaps uneasy visitor, encountering what is to them an unfamiliar environment. First evaluate the immediate impression they will gain from the entrance hall; is it welcoming? And when they have entered will they know where to go to get the information they require? Will the entrance hall be inviting and visually stimulating, celebrating children's achievement with lively displays of work strategically placed to intrigue them when they sit comfortably waiting to be received? Or will it be cluttered by the delivery of paper towels left over from the previous day? Will the work on the walls, if indeed there is any, be mounted neatly in a way that enhances the quality of the children's efforts? Will it be possible to work out who produced it and what has stimulated its creation? Indeed, does the entrance hall give a message that this is a school that cares?

This is only the start of your detective work in 'smelling a good school'. On taking a grand tour a visitor would hope to find positive clues to the 'creative climate' in the cleanliness and organisation of the learning environment, the way furniture has been arranged to encourage flexible learning, the state of fixtures, fittings and equipment, the systems operating which ensure that pupils can access materials independently, and of course the manner in which visual material is presented throughout the hall, corridors and in every classroom. They would draw conclusions from the care and consistency that had been taken in its presentation, as well as the quality of the outcomes. But, more importantly, these visual clues would be being read, not just by visitors, but intuitively by pupils as well. Therefore the 'creative climate' is an important dimension of the 'hidden curriculum'; their visual education is continually operating throughout the school environment, which if managed effectively becomes a practical example of the principles of good visual design. You may ask why this should be the specific concern of the hard pressed art and design subject leader, particularly if the role is not made explicit in your job description. It is because, whilst this is obviously the responsibility of everyone, the person charged with establishing and maintaining the 'creative climate' is the person who is by definition most visually aware. The buck stops with you, so see this as an opportunity to raise the status of the subject you lead and make sure it is a key strand in your development plan.

The challenge in reconciling differing staff perspectives
Establishing a general policy and the specific procedures that are to be adopted by all in the school can be more problematic than one might imagine. Be warned that, as someone who delivers a wide range of in-service training and who is regularly asked to run 'display courses' for subject leaders, I am often told that establishing a specific display policy can be one of the most contentious issues within a school

1

that they have met. This is because, in my experience, teachers tend to divide into two camps, with the views of the most extreme in each being difficult to reconcile. On the one hand some extremists believe that every school should have an absolutely clear set of rules for organisation of stimulus and presentation of pupils' work, which is adhered to by everyone, with the threat of draconian disciplinary measures being used against anybody who violates these divine precepts. At the other end of the spectrum is a conviction in some teachers that to be told how to display work in their classroom represents a violation of their human rights! The problems arise because, as in most aesthetic choices, there is no absolute right and wrong; the same 'lively' display created by one person is in another's eyes 'muddled'. One teacher's carefully 'low tone and discreet' choice of mounting paper is to another simply 'dull and boring'. And when a person's taste is questioned, or when, even worse, they are not permitted to exercise their personal choice because it is not in accord with agreed practice, they may become very resentful. But failing to meet this challenge to your leadership can create a presentational free-for-all that results in a chaotic visual jumble worse than the visual excesses of Piccadilly Circus.

So do not underestimate the pitfalls facing you if charged by the head teacher with reconciling these opposing viewpoints, but you should rise to the challenge

nevertheless. Maybe somewhere halfway along the continuum is the most secure position for the wise subject leader to establish their initial position?

A display policy summarised
It will now be clear that I prefer to take a broader view when influencing the 'creative climate' policy for the school, only one aspect of which will be the procedures for display. So there are likely to be some basic principles that everyone should be willing to sign up to initially, before focusing on the more specific and subjective aspects of display, and this is probably the right place to start if controversy is to be avoided initially. For instance no one would argue against consistent systems for organising resources and equipment throughout the school, as these will facilitate easy transfer from one class to another. Equally no teacher would suggest that schools should not be stimulating places visually. So as a corollary every classroom should have a range of exciting visual stimuli related to a particular topic, displayed in an inventive manner. Displaying the most ordinary objects in a new way, outside their normal environment, will draw attention to them, you will argue. If handling objects also can be encouraged, then their tactile as well as visual qualities can be explored, you can further suggest. Logically, the outcomes of pupils' work using these stimuli should be displayed alongside the artefacts in a way that enhances their creative efforts.

However when displaying pupils' work another controversial issue may arise. Which pupils' work is displayed? If only the 'best' work is put up (which is tempting as this will provide examples of best practice for others to emulate) some pupils will be disadvantaged, so all will agree it is important to ensure that at some time each child has some of their achievements celebrated publicly.

What is displayed is another important issue to be addressed in your policy. Most teachers will recognise that too much dense written work is visually unappealing, so will not be resistant to the proposition that a few carefully chosen quotations are preferable. And too much work displayed without any visual relief will confuse and exhaust the eye of the viewer; in a piece of music periods of silence are as important as the notes themselves. Neither would anyone challenge the view that unless displays are changed regularly they become part of the wallpaper, ending up being ignored by pupils, even if occasional inspectors are impressed.

If in accepting these and other broad principles every teacher is then allowed to display work in their own effective but individual way, they will not dramatically sully the whole school visual harmony, as long as this freedom is exercised only within classrooms, with a standardised approach reserved for the corridors, the school hall and other whole school displays. Whatever is eventually agreed should be written up as a basic policy,

…every classroom should have range of exciting visual stimuli related to a particular topic, displayed in an inventive manner.

with a set of advice and guidelines that will be added to your documentation as an appendix.

But your ambitions may be greater than this. You may wish to get everyone to agree to display everything in a consistent manner irrespective of whether it is in or outside the classroom. This is where each subject leader, who works with the people on the ground, will know how far they can go. Remember the head teacher of the school is also likely to have a view about the extent to which a display policy should be totally 'corporate' and enforced at the expense of individual flexibility, so they too should be involved in planning your strategy. Taking the head teacher along with you in your development strategy has been the watchword so far – and never more so than here.

So having pointed out the problems that may be faced when challenged to persuade all staff to adopt even some general principles, I can best illustrate the further difficulties that that may be encountered in establishing more specific rules by considering a simple display task, that of arranging several pieces of pupils' work with accompanying text on a wall. Inevitably my personal preferences will now become evident in this area, although I emphasise that I am not a hard-liner and I recognise it is not possible to prove that my way is the right way; of course there are no absolutes, but if you want one way of approaching this basic task, here are my methods.

The likely starting point for debate before this task even commences is to decide whether all pieces of work should be mounted, before considering how this procedure should be standardised across classrooms. Essentially I believe that all

work that is displayed in the classroom deserves to be presented with care, although I feel that the extreme of double mounting every piece of work is too time-consuming even if, as is now being advised, display work is to be done by a classroom assistant rather than the teacher. So everything should be mounted. The colour of the mount will need to be varied according to the colours of the piece of work that is being mounted; I prefer lower tone greys and beige papers, or black and white, perhaps picking up a colour theme from the pupils' creative efforts, rather than obtrusive mounts in the vivid or even fluorescent colours that could be chosen, because these in my view distract from the work itself.

I prefer about a centimetre border all the way round. Making several pieces of work, often of differing size, fit into a rectangular display board is the next problem. When displaying a number of two-dimensional pieces of work on a wall I find it helpful initially to mark out the dimensions of the vertical space on a flat horizontal area and lay out the work there so that it can be moved round easily in order to achieve a harmonious arrangement that fits, before finally putting it up on the wall. Be mindful of the childrens' eye level, as displays that are too high are difficult for small children to see.

How all pieces will be arranged is again a matter of debate but I always feel that if the outside edge of the total display echoes the rectangle of the space on which it is displayed any internal variations within the rectangle will not disturb the eye. The temptation to be 'original' or 'creative' in display, for instance in displaying the outcomes of a project on trees on a series of painted branches, is a risk, unless one

has the natural aptitude of a Harvey Nicholls window dresser. Thus I also dislike work that is displayed at an angle 'to make it interesting', and would expect that the dull beige display board on the wall would have been covered overall with a tasteful colour that highlights and complements the mounted pieces, rather than one that is highly contrasting, before individual pieces are arranged on top of it. In corridors, the long expanse of board can be broken up into sections using different colours and tones of backing paper to mark out sections.

Work needs to be fastened securely to the board of course, and I prefer a staple tacker to drawing pins, which can create a 'spotty' disturbing effect, though I'm always careful not to drive the tacks all the way into the board as they can be very difficult to dig out afterwards. Lettering for the display is important and with the introduction of ICT simple straightforward captions can be produced easily. Lettering styles should be simple and consistent throughout a display and I dislike freehand lettering, though recognise that some would say this is an opportunity to provide a handwriting exemplar to pupils. If display is not to be merely a way of enhancing the work or decorating the school, the display should challenge the viewer. Display titles that ask questions are preferable, for instance, rather than simply describing the content, as in 'Class two exercises in painting green'. I would favour the more thought provoking 'How many different greens can you see in the pictures painted by class two?' Obviously if the creative work has been inspired by stimulus material that can be displayed alongside pupil outcomes, then the display will be also more meaningful.

Illustrations 1-2 inclusive:
Classroom displays in primary schools

When it comes to displaying three-dimensional work, the average primary school will not have specialist three-dimensional display stands and will need to conscript boxes and tables that can be covered with fabric, which can be extended up the wall to change smoothly from the vertical to the horizontal – although sometimes displays incorporate such drapes as a convention rather than a need. Too many three-dimensional artefacts will create a cluttered effect and can be inconvenient in small primary classrooms but corners are useful places for such displays, because they are less obstructive when located there, and the eye is led naturally towards the central features. Displaying three-dimensional works from the ceiling is possible, though it may be regarded as a fire hazard, and can again generate an overhead and little noticed visual clutter, unless used with discretion.

That I can use up so much space simply discussing how pieces of work can be presented demonstrates how it is possible for complete manuals to be written on display practice. Such detail will be found in further reading suggested elsewhere. There are many aspects of this topic that I deal with on training sessions that I have not touched upon. For further detailed guidance try entering the words 'display' 'stimulus' and 'presentation' into the search engine on the NSEAD website **www.nsead.org**

The most important argument for addressing the issue of the 'creative climate' is that a school that has a cohesive policy put systematically into practice is not merely adopting a marketing strategy to create a good impression for outsiders. More significantly, by actively designing the pupils' visual environment, their visual education is being continually enhanced.

Staff Activity suggestion
In this short section I could not possibly cover every aspect of display theory and practice.

I have concentrated instead on the issues that arise when the subject leader decides to address the quality of the 'creative climate'. You will realise by now that you need to approach the introduction of a display policy tactfully. If every one in a school is to have a standardised approach there needs to be open discussion and careful negotiations with individual staff, so that all feel they have ownership of the general principles and, hopefully, the specific procedures. In this sense the same strategy that I outlined in an earlier section for corporately establishing the curriculum plan should be utilised by the subject leader to establish a policy for the schools 'creative climate'.

To encourage debate and stimulate thinking on my courses I provide a practical display that demonstrates these principles and provides an opportunity for all to criticise; why not try this at a development meeting at your school to introduce the topic? You will have to explain the reasons behind your model display in order to convince everyone the effort involved is worthwhile. Next divide the staff group into pairs and ask them each to study a display in their colleagues classroom and then share, first, what they think are its strengths and, second, say what they would change in order to improve it if the display was theirs.

ASSESSMENT

Chapter seven

It is apparent that assessment procedures in primary schools are often underdeveloped in art and design. The reasons for this will be considered in this chapter and some suggestions given that will guide the subject leader towards establishing a manageable assessment system.

Can art be assessed?

How often have I heard a teacher, usually with a little or no artistic training or background, state that 'art cannot be assessed'? Of course they are partly correct if they are comparing assessment in art and design with those subjects that, at the primary level, have a 'right or wrong' answer, such as in mathematics. They are only partly correct because there are actually aspects of art and design that do have a similar 'right or wrong' response – green is always produced by mixing blue and yellow and there are many aspects of art history that involve incorrigible data that can be remembered and tested. What these teachers are referring to though is the problem of assessing the outcomes of the creative process, which certainly do not have absolute measures by which one can assess them.

The fact that much of the output of artistic activity in schools cannot be measured in these absolute 'right or wrong' terms does lead to a view in the uninitiated that art cannot be assessed. But this view flies in the face of the established sophisticated procedures for assessing pupil achievement that are used at Key Stage 4,

where pupils are given examination grades in art and design which are rarely challenged. It does seem to be possible to assess the outcomes of art and design activities but not in the same way as achievement in which knowledge based subjects is evaluated.

The assessment of literacy and numeracy, using standard assessment tasks, concentrates on clear and measurable outcomes with the teacher's judgement not being involved. The unfortunate result of this can be that the measurable aspects of English, such as grammar and punctuation, are assessed at the expense of the creative writing dimension which involves judgement against agreed criteria. There is a possibility that the requirements of assessment may actually influence the content of what is taught in art and design in a similar manner, because it does seem that some aspects of the curriculum content and standards are easier than others to reach a common judgement about.

I illustrate this in my work with PGCE trainees by asking them to make judgments about a set of observational drawings in which each pupil has drawn the same object using one medium. Of course this activity is unrealistic in that one would not wish to assess individual pieces of work but rather the many outcomes of a particular project, but it serves to illustrate the dilemma of assessment. The group is required both to make judgements about the standards of each piece of work and also establish the criteria they are using to

make their judgments. As long as they know what the teacher asked the pupils to do – the aim of the activity – there is always a surprising degree of conformity in the judgments they make. However repeating that task with a more open-ended and creative exercise, concerned not simply with recording what pupils see but involving a degree of imaginative interpretation results in much greater disagreement.

Assessing the outcomes of the imaginative and expressive aspects of artistic activities with pupils may be more problematic but one would not want to exclude this vital dimension of the artistic process from the classroom for that reason. As observational work can be more convincingly assessed there is a danger that this could dominate the primary curriculum at the expense of open-ended and less easily assessed creative and imaginative projects. This is certainly the situation in the secondary school where the need to ensure that pupils have produced work that will gain high examination grades has meant that teachers have over-emphasised observational work at the expense of the imaginative. In some cases they have constrained opportunities for students to take risks and experience failure – an important aspect of the learning process. This is the assessment dilemma, which has similarities to teachers 'teaching to the test' in primary school literacy activities, to the detriment of the creative writing process. Although primary school assessment is certainly underdeveloped at present, and there is much that could

> **Staff development activity**
> To involve staff in establishing assessment criteria repeat the student exercise I have described earlier with the staff group.
>
> Remember the now familiar key characteristics of assessment for learning in the core subjects published by the DfES. Assessment for learning requires the sharing of learning objectives with pupils, helping pupils to know and recognise the standards they are aiming for, involves pupils in peer and self assessment, provides feedback which enables pupils to recognise their next steps and how to take them, promotes confidence that every pupil can approve and involves both teacher and pupil reviewing and reflecting on assessment information.
>
> As a second staff exercise you should consider collectively how these principles might usefully be applied to art and design without producing a system that is so onerous it will not be used.

be done to make it more systematic, the wise subject leader should be wary of establishing an assessment driven art and design curriculum in the primary years that could constrain the breadth of curriculum experience.

A manageable assessment policy
Unless it is aspects of absolute artistic knowledge, such as factual art history, whatever is being assessed in art and design involves judgment. If clear criteria are agreed between teacher and examinations board, or indeed teacher and pupil, the teacher can make judgments using these criteria which, though they are of course subjective, can through moderation procedures generate a surprising degree of consensus.

Practical assessment procedures in art and design must therefore have clearly established assessment criteria that are published in the staff art and design handbook and are used throughout the school. The most obvious criteria to utilise are the English National Curriculum levels, which are available to assess the body of individual pupils' work at the end of Key Stages 1 and 2. A scrutiny of these levels will reveal that they are daunting in their complexity. It is possible to break down these National Curriculum levels into three clear and discrete strands, and this makes them much easier to use as a tool for pupil assessment.

There are a number of other features of a strategy for effective assessment of art and design that should be instituted by the proactive subject leader. A folder of work can be gathered together which illustrates standards related to particular levels. Collating this could be a useful staff activity if all staff bring work to a staff meeting and decide whether the work is of a standard **below, in line with** or **above** a particular level. Such a developing resource can be used to establish standards where there is disagreement about the level a pupil has achieved and will establish a benchmark for all.

Repeating pieces of work at various stages during the lifetime of a pupil in their primary school career will also be revealing. This can be done in a sketchbook that might then be passed to the secondary school on transition as a helpful record of their progress and attainment. Keeping examples of pupils' work in a portfolio throughout their time in the primary school is also desirable; even bulky three-dimensional work can now be photographed using the school digital camera. All this work can be recorded on CD, again to be passed to the secondary school as an invaluable record of pupils' development.

Effective assessment in art and design must take place sensitively, with the teacher discussing with the pupil what they have achieved, evaluating the strengths and weaknesses of the process

of their visual enquiry and the outcomes, considering the extent to which pupils have met the aims of the set task, and even setting targets for improvement, in the same way that it is done for the 'academic' subjects. Written comments are preferable to inscrutable marks. Pupils can be encouraged to participate in their own assessment procedures if the subject leader breaks down their curriculum plan into what pupils should know and be able to do at the end of each year. When they agree with the teacher that the standard has been reached they can check it off on their self-assessment sheet. Joint assessment between pupils is invaluable. At key points in the creation of their work they can be required to decide in pairs what is the best feature of their friends' work, and state what they would do to improve it if it was theirs.

EXPLORING CONNECTIONS BETWEEN ART & DESIGN AND LITERACY & NUMERACY

Chapter eight

1

It has been pointed out in chapter one that literacy and numeracy have for some time been prioritised in the primary curriculum, many would argue to the disadvantage of art and design. However the proactive subject leader can capitalise on this fact rather than bemoan its impact by demonstrating how the subject can positively contribute to pupils' development in both these key aspects of their learning. If practice in both the theoretical and practical aspects of art and design is seen to regularly address literacy and numeracy, the subject will gain status, even with those who have a degree of scepticism about the value of more expressive activities. Therefore exploiting the following ways in which direct links can be made with literacy and numeracy is a sensible strategy.

Art and design and literacy

In every primary classroom, art and design work on the walls is likely to be presented with its title alongside the name of the young artist who has produced it – so as to challenge their imagination always encourage pupils to devise their own original titles. All staff should also be encouraged to present key words adjacent to the work that relate to its production. For instance it could be that the stated aim of the work was 'exploring the visual element of line' or it might be noted that 'water colour paint is transparent but powder paint is opaque when it is dry'. In this way pupils' verbal vocabulary will be developed in concert with their visual understanding.

CHAPTER EIGHT
Exploring connections between art & design
and literacy & numeracy

PAGE 31

…if practice in both theoretical and practical aspects of art and design is seen to regularly address literacy and numeracy, the subject will be given status, even with those who have a degree of scepticism about the value of more expressive activities.

Critical studies activities should be both theoretical and practical. Verbal exchanges, developing vocabulary and language, are just as important as the related practical activity. Pupils therefore should be encouraged to critically evaluate the work of mature artists and their own personal creative efforts. This can be done in a variety of ways. It may be that critical analysis takes place during a whole class discussion, when pupils both express their preferences about a range of differing works of art and, more importantly, make aesthetic judgements and give reasons for their statements, which can later be recorded alongside the reproductions. When challenging pupils to appraise their own work I find it very helpful regularly to encourage pupils at the end of the lesson to exchange their art work with that of another pupil. Ask each to give the other one their opinion on both what they feel is the best feature of the work and what they would do to improve it if the work was their own. As each will express a view about the other's work whilst having their own work criticised by their companion, sensitive and carefully expressed judgments usually prevail!

If pupils are to use sketchbooks effectively they should write notes in them about what they see as well as recording visual experiences using artistic media. Though one would not want written notes in sketchbooks to be corrected in the same way that other more formal writing might be, key words can be reinforced by the teacher when they are encountered.

There is a range of practical ways of linking literacy with art and design if the teacher is inventive. For instance it is possible to give pupils words such as smooth, rough, scratchy and interconnected and ask them to make a symbolic response in clay. Words and pictures can be integrated in posters, juxtaposed using ICT for illustrative purposes, or the names of pieces that have been cast in plaster incised into the surface before it dries.

Art and design and numeracy
The potential for linking art and design with numeracy is enormous. The systematic rhythms and forms of nature and their underlying mathematical structures have

proved a rich stimulus for artists. For instance Leonardo da Vinci's sketchbook shows how the artist evolved some of his mechanical structures from a study of grasses. Introduce pupils also to the Golden Mean and Fibonacci to illustrate the relationship between mathematical sequences and natural forms. Many paintings rely upon numerical systems for their composition, as in the use of the Golden Section. A study of the work of the Bauhaus or the geometric art of the 1960s will also be fruitful. Practical art activities, particularly those using three-dimensional materials can be structured to challenge pupils to measure accurately.

To focus more specifically on numeracy, a perusal of many contemporary art forms illustrated in books and visits to galleries will reveal their enormous potential as a basis for activities in numeracy and practical art and design. By showing pupils works by artists such as Victor Vasarely and the 'Op' artists, Sol LeWitt and Eduardo Paolozzi which are often based on a symmetrical mathematical grid, similar regular patterned collages can be produced using different geometric gummed shapes. Practical activities can also include making tessellation patterns, using the many large-scale geometric sculptural works of contemporary sculptors as a basis for small-scale clay structures (see for example

Tony Smith or Max Bill), or draw round overlapping large cardboard cut-out circles squares and triangles to produce dynamic geometric patterns after studying Frank Stella's work.

Making mobiles similar to those of Alexander Calder will require an understanding of balance, as well as careful measurement. Pupils can construct a large-scale lightweight triangular based pyramid. Each pupil will produce their own regular tetrahedron pyramid from 6 pieces of dowel, each 2 ft long. Arrange 35 of these in layers (1, 3, 6, 10, 15: triangular numbers) starting with the largest layer, and joining pieces together using elastic bands or wire garden ties. For older and

more able pupils consider a project on 'making connections' using their sketchbooks and the digital camera. Challenge them to record natural forms and other phenomena that demonstrate properties such as symmetry and repeating patterns, related manufactured structures and objects that replicate the patterns they have noted in nature. For instance ripples in water might be juxtaposed with undulating patterns in roof tiles; the spiral of a shell connected to a spiral staircase, etc. These sketch book studies can then be developed into larger works.

CHAPTER EIGHT
Exploring connections between art & design
and literacy & numeracy

PAGE 33

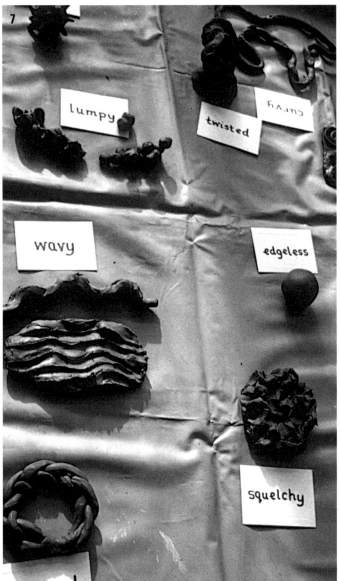

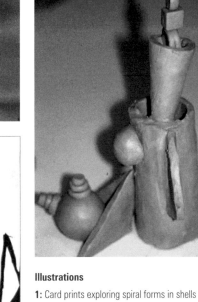

Illustrations

1: Card prints exploring spiral forms in shells

2: Painting Tessellated patterns onto a cotton sheet

3: The sheets draped over young pupils to create a tessellated dragon

4: Tesselated potato print patterns

5: Integrating words with cast body parts

6: 'Who can roll the longest sausage in clay? Is it as tall as me?'

7: A symbolic visual response to keywords using clay

8: Exploring symmetry and reflection

9: Building a pyramid out of dowel rod – teachers' INSET

10: Pupils respond to work of art by Howard Hodgkin in words and paintings

11: Small-scale clay models using geometrical forms

SECTION TWO ESSENTIAL INFORMATION ON KEY CONTENT, MEDIA AND PROCESSES

THE VISUAL ELEMENTS AND VISUAL ENQUIRY

Chapter nine

The subject leader who has followed a course of artistic study to A level GCE standard is likely to have a reasonable knowledge of the visual elements of art and design. Not all staff will possess such an understanding and many will need much support if they are to introduce pupils to the language of art. The visual elements are an essential tool for developing visual awareness and one strand of your curriculum plan should address the visual elements. This chapter offers a strategy for their development in your school.

What is the visual vocabulary of art?
The visual vocabulary of art can be likened to the development of vocabulary in the teaching of English language. The making of a work of art in two or three-dimensions involves the use of different aspects of the visual elements. These include line, colour, texture, pattern and shape, tone and three-dimensional space and form. Perceptive teachers can make pupils aware of the language of the elements, which will develop and extend their personal 'visual vocabulary' and increase the expressive capacity of their work.
The origins of the visual element concept can be found in the innovative work of the Bauhaus, which was further developed by Maurice de Sausmarez and the basic design education movement of the 1960s. Most recently the influential primary books available from NSEAD, written by Nigel Meager [1], focus on strategies that develop

pupils' understanding of the visual elements, in a series of interesting projects.

Starting with an observed source
The most usual way of introducing primary pupils to the visual elements is to develop their understanding by using a first-hand observational source, rather than starting with the total abstraction of 'basic design' activities. The teacher should focus on subject matter that provides appropriate challenges. For example, children will learn how to represent changes in surface in a group of still life bottles and vases by using light and shade in pencils of differing degrees of hardness with increasing

subtlety. Or how to enrich the drawing of a bird by concentrating on ways of representing the soft texture of the feathers – or perhaps by examining closely the full range of colours in an object by mixing all the colours they can find in it.

Visual enquiry and the sketchbook
The teacher can ask pupils to look at a natural object selectively, and concentrate on its pattern and texture, or reduce a manufactured structure to simple flat pattern by challenging pupils to concentrate their visual exploration on the shapes between the forms as a specific exercise. It can be helpful to take an observed

…the visual elements are an essential tool for developing visual awareness.

source and analyse it systematically in a sequence of drawings, concentrating successively on its linear qualities, its colour, its texture or pattern and this is a good way of using the sketchbook as a source of visual exploration. Establishing a sketchbook and using it in part to explore the visual elements is important. Remember it should be used as a visual journal rather than a drawing book. Pupils should be encouraged to gather within it new source materials to stimulate the development of ideas and to make collages of textured rubbings and experiments with colour. Brief visual notes and even written comments are as important as careful recording. Pupils should also be encouraged to collect small-scale samples from the environment, which focus on particular aspects of the visual elements as source material; for example, a fading autumn leaf collected because of its colour scheme or a weathered piece of paper as a record of a particular textured feature. These can be stuck into the sketchbook as part of their reference collection. The sketchbook might even be constructed for a range of innovative media; it could be in a box or be a videotape record. Pupils should also be challenged to find and record in their sketchbook aspects of the visual environment which concentrate on line, colour or pattern and so on, to build up their own visual vocabulary reference book which could be divided into sections according to the differing visual elements.

Linking the visual elements with media
Each of the visual elements has associations with a particular medium. Some non-specialists may find it less confusing and easier to understand if your curriculum plan centres work with a particular medium alongside a particular visual element; there is a traditional relationship between, for instance, drawing and line and tone, painting and colour, printmaking with the exploration of surface and texture, clay and three-dimensional materials with space and form even though many art activities with media involve an interaction of all of the visual elements. For example drawings can be coloured and printmaking can explore pattern as well as texture, and a collage could combine aspects of several of the visual elements. Form and space can only be fully understood through practical activities in three dimensions.

Knowledge of the visual elements
Some aspects of learning related to the visual elements involve specific and measurable knowledge and can thus be taught specifically and progressively as explained in detail in an earlier section on curriculum planning; for instance pupils need to understand that primary colours cannot be mixed, but that two primary colours when mixed make a secondary one, that there are warm and cold colours but that some greens may be warm or cool depending on the relative amounts of blue and yellow that are used to mix them, or that complementary colours are

strongly contrasting and will be found as opposite partners on a colour wheel. Rather than teaching this mechanically though, pupils need to be given the opportunity to experiment with media to discover from themselves the 'rules' of colour, and experience through the creative process the production of harmonious or visually dynamic art works. Ultimately there is no right and wrong answer in much visual elements activity; though pupils can learn the language in English in order to express themselves correctly, a piece of writing involves originality and creativity which unlike grammar does not adhere to absolute rules. It is the same in much visual elements learning, so pupils should be encouraged to critically evaluate their personal efforts and teachers must develop skill in questioning them in order to extend their awareness. For instance they should ask pupils to look closely at a natural form and describe how many different sorts of line they can find to draw using appropriate media to compare thick lines with thin, hard with soft and furry with crisp.

Extending understanding of the visual elements through studying the work of other artists, craftspersons and designers
Much can be learnt about the visual elements by a study of the work of artists, craftspeople and designers. Although all art involves the use of the visual elements some 'Modern Art' in the early 20th century was concerned specifically with taking an observed visual starting point

and 'abstracting' from it, systematically reducing the observed source to its basic visual elements, so that its origin was sometimes no longer recognisable.

A study of the art of this period as part of your critical studies programme will develop an understanding of the visual elements. Other artists, particularly those working in the 1960s, were occupied with manipulating the visual elements to produce an art work that was visually pleasing and stimulating, without an observed starting point, and thus totally 'abstract' in conception as well as execution. Therefore in critical studies activities it is possible to select some works of art for use with children in both these categories, and to ask pupils to concentrate their discussion on describing and analysing the starting points, the qualities of the colour scheme, or the pattern and composition, as a way of extending their understanding of the visual elements. An examination of the work of some of the key artists who have centred their activities on aspects of the visual elements should be incorporated systematically into the school scheme of work, with large scale reproduction examples purchased as part of the central critical studies resource bank. There are numerous possibilities. Pablo Picasso and Henri Matisse could be selected to focus on methods of developing an observed source into pattern and colour, and Graham Sutherland also developed twisted root forms into abstract symbolic shapes; Victor Pasmore progressively reduced environmental forms into pure abstraction and Henry Moore simplified and stylised the human form in his large scale sculpture. However other artists such as Patrick Heron explored colour and pattern for its own sake, as did Victor Vasarely, and Bridget Riley in their hard-edged optical patterning. Alexander Calder, Laszlo Moholy Nagy and Anthony Caro were concerned with purely abstract three-dimensional forms, exploring abstract concepts such as balance and spatial relationships.

[1] See 'Teaching Art at Key Stage 1' and 'Teaching Art at Key Stage 2' available from NSEAD publications.

4

Staff development activities

Non-specialist teachers in primary schools understandably may be hesitant and unconfident in relation to dealing with such artists, because of their limited personal artistic background. It is important to recognise that the best way to develop an understanding of the vocabulary of art is through engagement in practical activities, so an in-service training session which focuses on using media to extend teachers ability in using charcoal to explore line and tone, paint to explore colour, or clay to express form, is always helpful. But why not be more innovative and have a staff meeting in an art gallery, using the education officer to explain the content of some of the more abstract works before engaging in a practical project based upon them?

Illustrations

1: Exploring tone by drawing white painted objects
2: Developing an understanding of the visual elements by using a first-hand observational source
3: Using the sketchbook as a source of visual inspiration
4: Collage combining aspects of the visual elements
5: Texture and colour experiments in a sketchbook
6: Understanding form and space
7: Exploring primary colours
8: Exploring secondary colours
9: Pattern and shape in three-dimensional construction work
10: Discovering the 'rules' of colour

CRITICAL AND CULTURAL STUDIES

Chapter ten

Art activities in primary schools are predominantly practical in nature. This traditional approach is based on the philosophy of writers such as Herbert Read whose model for art education was the 'child as artist'. However when your pupils finish their education only a small number will go to art school and even fewer will be artists – the large majority eventually will be consumers of art and design rather than practitioners.

Thus, though personal growth is certainly one key aim of art and design education, the subject is also concerned with educating pupils to make informed aesthetic choices in later life – in selecting art, making fashion choices and design decisions. Though this facility may in part be achieved by involvement in the practice of art, a number of major art educators such as Elliot Eisner have questioned the extent to which a practical art programme can address effectively this development of pupils' 'critical and cultural abilities'. Eisner argued that the visual arts curriculum was '…highly saturated with activities that involve the youngsters in the making of art forms' and stated that the curriculum should be concerned '…not only with the productive domain but also the critical and historical domains as well. Since the English National Art Curriculum included such activities as 'critical discussion', 'learning about the work of other artists', and 'evaluating the work of others', critical and cultural studies have become a regular feature

of the programme of art and design work. This chapter considers the implications of critical studies in the primary school.

Making critical studies meaningful

It is now generally accepted that it is the teacher's task to provide an opportunity for experiences that cater for the development of the pupils' visual awareness and discrimination. Though the central thrust of art and design activities in most primary schools at present continues to concentrate on practical work with a range of media, pupils now more commonly explore the relationship between their own practice and their appreciation and knowledge of established works of art, craft and design. As subject leader you will want to address this area of activity but though it will not seem problematic to someone with an art background, the less experienced teacher can find the requirement daunting. As a consequence, in many schools, such teachers tend to choose safe and easily accessible critical studies sources. For instance it is common to find children making a self-portrait being influenced by Picasso, exploring optical colour mixing through looking at Georges Seurat or developing and using Paul Klee's stylised fish as a basis for their collage work. These examples may be typical of the range of mature artists I see often used in primary schools – just some of the usual suspects in a rather too narrow range.

Though there is an understandable tendency for non-art specialist teachers to concentrate on artworks in their teaching

that they personally enjoy and are familiar with, it is important for the subject leader to ensure that there is not an over concentration on the familiar and predictable. The programme should be broad and balanced covering a wide range of both artists and designers from a range of different genres, periods and cultures with no evident gender bias. The works of male artists and sculptors from Northern Europe in the late nineteenth and early twentieth century should not dominate the programme.

Critical studies – the verbal dimension

Critical studies activities should be a normal feature of the large majority of projects in the primary school and talking about artworks and making art should be interactive. Pupils should always be encouraged to formulate their views about art works, express a balanced and reasoned opinion and recognise that there are alternative perspectives for analysis. In the first instance, when faced with a work of art they may make immediate arbitrary choices about what they like and dislike; though these opinions are of course entirely valid, these preferences are not necessarily judgements in which aesthetic values are involved. A framework can be introduced to the debate and developed by the teacher through skilful questioning, which will encourage pupils to understand the difference between these arbitrary choices and the making of informed aesthetic judgements. One can, for instance, consider the subject matter systematically: the way the artist has

…critical discussion, learning about the work of other artists, and evaluating the work of others – critical and cultural studies – have become a regular feature of the programme of art and design work.

used the medium; the visual elements content; or the message communicated by the work of art in order to produce a more coherent debate. A number of models for such activity have been presented which divide aesthetic judgements into discrete categories to assist the teacher in guiding pupils through the process. The subject leader might profitably consider this activity for a staff meeting or a training day, because it is important that teachers themselves also develop personal confidence in making a balanced aesthetic evaluation of diverse art works and artefacts, recognising that the aim of critical studies activity is not to inculcate pupils into the good taste of the teacher but to encourage pupils to think for themselves, justify their judgements and discriminate perceptively.

The most appropriate teaching style for such critical and cultural studies is a non-academic and interactive one; if critical studies activity is presented as 'art history' it may become predominantly knowledge-based, which could disadvantage the less able. As in all aspects of primary activity the written word should be seen as only one form of expression and pupils should have an opportunity to engage in the critical process inclusively.

Critical studies and practical work
The other complementary strand in critical studies activities is in the relationship the teacher establishes between pupils' own practice and their appreciation and knowledge of established works of art,

craft and design. Though basing pupils' practical work on the work of mature artists and designers can produce interesting and exciting results it is important to avoid direct copying – this is not the most productive way to develop pupils' critical abilities given the limited time available for the subject in schools. A typical example is the direct copy of a reproduction of Vincent Van Gogh's painting of Sunflowers; rather than this, teachers should be encouraged to discuss his use of colour, and possibly ask pupils to experiment on a small scale with some of the ways in which he applied paint or laid certain colours next to one another. This could be done using pupils' sketchbooks, before returning to first hand observation of sunflowers, set up perhaps as a Van Gogh still life for pupils' large scale practical activities.

There are numerous other approaches that avoid direct copying. Consider making a three-dimensional version in clay of a two-dimensional image or turn an original drawing into a three-dimensional environment hanging from the ceiling, extend pupils' use of media by studying the way the artist has applied paint, explore the visual elements through a study of an artist by adopting their particular colour scheme, reproduce the art work but change the artist's viewpoint – the potential is limitless. Equally every general primary topic will provide an opportunity for a critical and cultural studies reference and maybe some related practical work. A project on bicycles could feature Ferdinand Leger and

Jean Metzinger; a sea theme could produce a three-dimensional octopus after looking at the work of Utagawa Kuniyoshi and Kawanabe Kyosai – or enable pupils to work from digital photographs of themselves asleep in deckchairs in the style of Beryl Cook. One on transport could look at the Futurists or Tony Cragg's towers made from cars; the theme of water might lead to experimentation with the way that Helen Frankenthaler poured thin veils of colour onto raw canvas; or, as a group project, a Grecian topic could lead to the recreation of part of the Elgin frieze from the Parthenon as plaster cast from clay.

Resources
To facilitate such diverse activities the subject leader will wish to develop a large bank of visual resources and this resource requirement should feature as a regular strand in your development plan, with some resources being purchased each year from the art funds allocated by the head teacher. One of the reasons that a narrow range of critical studies references is often presented to pupils in schools arises from limitations in these visual resources. Therefore they must be of an adequate scale, particularly for whole class teaching, and if possible your collection should include original works, even if they are only generously donated by minor local artists. The selection should reflect the wide range of possible approaches and sources mentioned earlier, and need to be on a scale large enough to facilitate whole-class teaching. Reproductions need to be kept in large

plastic wallets to withstand wear from enthusiastic use, and are best kept centrally; the subject leader will need to establish a system to ensure that they can track their location after they have been borrowed by acquisitive individual teachers to support particular projects. There are now also countless web sites that provide examples of the work of artists and designers and it will assist busy colleagues if the appendix to your documentation includes references to these.

Artists in school

Artists in school also can do much to stimulate exciting critical studies activity but do remember that they are not art and design supply teachers. Their work with pupils should focus on de-coding their own practice as an artist – this after all is their raison d'être. It is important therefore that you are absolutely clear about what you want to achieve from having an artist in school, and consult staff to ensure that they have ownership of the placement. Prepare the artist carefully in advance to ensure that materials are available and the artist recognises the previous experience of pupils in the school. An artist may not be familiar with the normal rhythms of the school day nor be a natural communicator with young children, so advanced preparation and planning with them is vital if the event is to be successful. There maybe funding currently available to assist in artist placements and the current Creative Partnerships initiative from Arts Council England is centred on this type of activity but in view of the limited funds in the primary school you will need to make a judgement about the relative cost of having an artist in school when compared with purchasing longer term resources.

Using art galleries

Though critical and cultural studies activities cannot be addressed comprehensively by artists in schools, they can provide an exciting stimulus for a special project. Another resource is an exhibition in a local gallery which can be an exciting source of inspiration for the primary pupil but the subject leader must select the exhibition wisely and plan the event carefully. I can illustrate this by describing an excellent example centred upon an exhibition by the Scottish artist Alan Davie at the Mercer Gallery in Harrogate. Alan Davie established his major international reputation in the 1960s as an abstract expressionist, but his current work makes use of Celtic, Aboriginal and Egyptian symbols and incorporates incantations.

The subject leader of Hookstone Chase primary school in Harrogate, Christine Woodard, was seeking an artist whose work would be the mainspring for their annual art day, during which all pupils throughout the school engage in a range of art and design activities around a theme. She attended the teachers' preview having sensibly ensured that the gallery knew her commitment to such events in advance. Once there she sought the information pack which offered detailed information and additional workshops in aspects of Davie's work. Though his paintings are complex and abstract she saw enormous potential for a range of ways of working with pupils in her school. Pupils from Years 2 and 4 were taken to the exhibition and engaged in a workshop activity. Because of the limited practical facilities common in many galleries, with the assistance of the gallery staff she concentrated on simple recording activities that would familiarise the pupils with the artist's

work. Many of the children had not visited an art gallery before and this novelty, together with the large scale of the paintings with their vigorous style, bold colours and symbolic patterning excited them. Even very young pupils made detailed sketches, and discussed what the pictures represented to them and why they preferred one to another. Many of the pupils saw circles, spirals and cog shapes in the imagery, and talked about the pictures' inner movement and energy; their imaginations were in overdrive.

Back in the school, as the preparatory work for the art day commenced, three distinct themes emerged. Foundation and Key Stage 1 began to work on the concept of colour and pattern, and lower Key Stage 2 focused on the ideas of magic and magical signs. Christine, aware of a group of older Key Stage 2 boys who were not particularly keen on art, made a connection with Design and Technology by setting this group the problem of using motors to spin discs, animating the cogs and wheels they saw in the pictures. Initial ideas were explored through a range of two and three-dimensional media.

On art and design day all pupils worked together, each producing a one-class piece as well as smaller pieces. Reception children had tremendous fun creating shapes and patterns from classroom equipment to produce a relief picture with moving parts. Year 4 pupils, who had identified map like features in the artist's work made a 'Hogwarts' type train which would move on a magnet through a magical landscape. Upper Key Stage 2 pupils were absorbed in attaching motors to discs, and experimenting to see which colours and shapes would be most

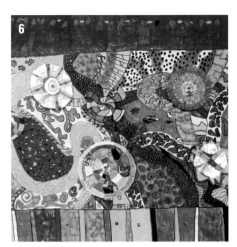

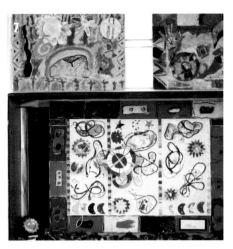

Illustrations

1-3: Children at an exhibition of the paintings of Alan Davie at Harrogate Art Gallery

4-9: Work by primary pupils stimulated by a visit to the exhibition at the gallery

effective when spinning. Others were involved in making circuits to illuminate areas covered with coloured cellophane. The outcomes were as diverse as they were dynamic.

This project exemplified good practice in the area of critical studies with primary pupils. Though these works were complex, Christine demonstrated that rare ability of the exceptional primary subject leader in making complicated artistic concepts accessible to young pupils. To celebrate the school's commitment to the subject, the 'art day' provided a long period of concentrated activity supplementing the pupil's regular art and design diet. The subject leader carefully prepared the event, working in concert with the art gallery staff. The direct experience of the paintings during the art gallery visit was supplemented by the reproductions that were taken back to the school for reference. These were not copied but rather used as a mainspring for a range of innovative approaches with diverse and individualised outcomes. She ensured that all staff members were involved and the profile of art and design was raised throughout the school with teachers, pupils and parents.

Staff development activities
As subject leader you will want to ensure that critical and cultural studies are meaningfully presented to pupils. Recognising the potential of such activities is vital, but also be aware of the possibility of trivialising of art and design sources because inexperienced colleagues misunderstand the reasons for such activities. Devoting a complete training day to sharing the outcomes from successful projects such as that I have described will be of assistance, particularly if you can involve a local gallery education officer and maybe a future artist in residence who could discuss their work and possible involvement with several year groups.

How your broad programme of critical studies is established and its delivery monitored, depends on the context in individual schools but one aspect of your scheme of work should include a 'map' to ensure that the coverage is broad rather than narrow or repetitive throughout the primary key stages. This needs to be established with sensitivity because teachers in your school may have favourite artists, who they have used in past projects, and they may be resistant to change. Therefore you might take the opportunity on this training day to ask staff to itemise the critical and cultural references that have featured in their class teaching programme in the past year. It will then be evident where there are overlaps and repetitions, where the range needs to be broadened and where some positive planning for the future can take place.

DRAWING

Chapter eleven

1

Many art and design educators regard drawing as a particularly important activity. Yet it is one that many non-specialists regard as the most difficult one to teach, largely because they feel they lack the expertise to engage in successful observational activity which they consider is the main aim of drawing. Taking a broader view of its functions can increase confidence. For though its use for recording the visual world is significant it is not exclusive; after all painting and three-dimensional work can also involve close observation and recording. Drawing is a key aspect of primary art and design activity that is considered in this chapter.

Definition and function
Actually defining drawing is quite difficult, as I have discovered during heated discussions with teachers on CPD training days. Though most would agree it is a graphic activity some have argued that one can 'draw in space with wire' or 'draw in clay'. Though philosophically this may be correct, this would seem to me to be too erudite a debate to be helpful if you are attempting to develop awareness of the benefits of drawing with less confident members of staff. There is no other area of art and design activity that generates such resistance in the uninitiated and teachers will need much support. In order to assist and develop the confidence of staff members who have had bad experiences in the past with insensitive teachers and who may instantly state

that they 'cannot draw', clear advice and guidance on the use of a range of drawing materials should be provided in the Appendix of your art and design staff handbook.

Observational activities
Teachers wish to support pupils in their observational work and there are a number of aids that will help pupils in the process without the teacher being required to demonstrate to pupils thus revealing what they perceive as their personal limitations. For instance magnifying glasses are useful to facilitate close observation. It is also important that the subject matter for this activity is interesting and centres on first hand sources. Observational drawing also often involves the representation of a three-dimensional object as a two-dimensional form and this is a skill that can involve the use of perspective. However perspective should not be taught mechanically, but introduced when it is required by older primary pupils who are engaged in directly drawing subject matter that can be most effectively represented by using it. It should be recognised that perspective is a Western artistic convention and that there are many other ways of representing space and depth in a drawing. Celebrating children's achievements and personal forms of expression in drawing, as in all art activity, is preferable to attempting to get them to work to preconceived adult conceptions and conventions, or copying from second hand sources. If this is done children

will enjoy producing very detailed drawings of complex objects from an early age without inhibition.

Some other important functions of drawing
In addition to observing and recording, drawing fulfils other artistic other functions. Each one is equally important, and if all are utilised then drawing can operate across the model for art activity that was described earlier in this handbook. It can be used to explore the visual elements, often concentrating on the use of line and tone, but a drawing can also be in colour, and pattern and space can be explored as well. Remember too that the teacher can develop observational activities into imaginative interpretations, or drawings may be stimulated directly from an imaginative source. A study of the drawing styles of mature artists will lead to critical appreciation and pupils can simultaneously develop their critical vocabulary and literacy skills by selecting appropriate words to describe the qualities of their drawings and the subject matter. Drawing has also a key role in the design process, involving the exploration and realisation of ideas in a variety of different ways, with work often taking place in sketchbooks. This full spectrum of drawing activities should be covered but, although drawing is an important process, pupils must also paint, print and engage in three-dimensional activities as a broad experience is important particularly as these other processes involve some drawing anyway. One can

...drawing is a key aspect of art and design activity.

draw with a paintbrush, for instance, and mono printing can promote a free form of graphic work. A review of drawing activities will also reveal that it is used in other curriculum areas and so it is important to ensure there is a balance between these activities and other aspects of the art and design curriculum.

Materials and processes
A bewilderingly wide range of drawing materials is available for use but pupils should be encouraged to explore the properties of each one in order to develop some skill in the selected medium. Avoid providing too many drawing materials at one time. What then are the essential drawing materials for general use in the primary classroom? The ordinary pencil is actually quite a sophisticated tool. Ensure that staff understand that pencils are made in different degrees of hardness which, if fully exploited, will provide a wide tonal range from subtle pale greys to deep blacks. Pupils should recognise the potential of pencils and master their use. Other related drawing media should not be ignored however. Each has unique properties. Even the humble felt-tip pen can produce bright colours and crisp lines.

Charcoal is an excellent cheap graphic material, ideal for working on a large scale. It favours a broader approach than the pencil and is a flexible and expressive medium. Experiment with smudging with paper or cloth, or drawing back into the grey charcoal surface with a soft rubber.

Encourage children to deliberately smudge the white paper surface to create a range of grey tones in order to do this. Compressed charcoal and charcoal pencils are now available that are certainly less messy, but whatever is used it will be essential to 'fix' the work with a spray fixative to avoid smudging when it is finished (this should be done by the teacher in a well ventilated space). Though charcoal is usually black, it can be combined with white chalk, or with different coloured chalk pastels to produce coloured drawings. Good-quality drawing paper, ranging from smooth to heavily textured, in different colours, will extend the possibilities of all drawing media, but is particularly important if the maximum impact is to be gained from the use of either pencil or charcoal.

In the last few years a range of more sophisticated pastels have come onto the market, each of which have different properties and these are a rich addition to the range of drawing media available. These include oil pastels, which will not mix with water but are of an especially intense hue. Try experimenting with scratching through thick layers of pastel to reveal the surface underneath, and remember they can mix like normal oil paints by working one colour on top of another. There are now also water-based pastels that can be used as a normal coloured drawing medium, but when water is added with a brush these will mix to produce a subtle watercolour effect.

Indeed watercolour itself can be added to a pencil drawing using a 'wash' technique to add colour to the line drawing. Coloured inks combine drawing and painting methods using different tools. As soon as one recognises that one can draw with a stick dipped in ink, or that scraper board or 'crayon etching' are also forms of drawing activity, it will soon become a less forbidding process.

There are of course more sophisticated drawing materials which can be introduced in Key Stage 2, such as conté crayons or graphite sticks, and the use of drawing in ICT is now common, but here I have only summarised a basic entitlement for pupils. Your curriculum plan should record when a particular medium is to be introduced and what children should learn about its properties and potential. Whatever is selected, it is important to provide a systematic programme if pupils are to develop their drawing confidence and expertise as they proceed through the school.

Drawing and sketchbooks

Children should be encouraged to draw at every opportunity and the process should be used freely for visual enquiry whenever an opportunity presents itself. Sketchbooks should be provided and pupils encouraged to use them regularly. These should be developed as visual notebooks where pupils use drawing as a creative tool, not just for carefully observed recording but as form of creative visual note taking.

The progress that a pupil is making in drawing can sometimes be most evident when viewing the contents of sketchbooks so, if possible, these should be retained when full. Sketchbooks should not be used solely as a record of observational drawing activities though. The 'sketch book' could be a box containing pieces collected from the environment which have interesting visual properties. Experiments in using drawing can be combined with paint; drawings can be digitally photographed and worked into using a program such as PhotoShop, and the outcomes developed as a collage, then perhaps used for further drawing activity. This 'sketch box' may contain collected imagery selected from magazines or a videotape record of a visual journey. If pupils are encouraged to draw regularly from an early age and incorporate drawing into a range of their art and design activities they will not become self-conscious about the outcomes as they grow older, and this confidence will be an asset as they face the challenges of secondary school.

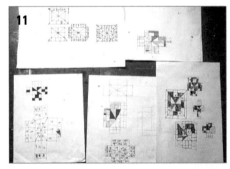

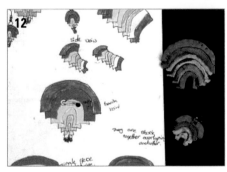

Some excellent and inexpensive booklets on drawing are published by 'Drawing Power', the education element of the Campaign for Drawing.

Illustrations

1-4: Observational drawing activity
5-6: Drawing to explore the visual elements
7-9: Imaginative drawings
10-12: Drawings in sketchbooks
13: A mono print drawing
14-17: Experimenting with drawing media

PAINT

Skills in painting will only develop effectively if the teacher introduces painting tools and media systematically, and encourages pupils to experiment, providing learning tasks that are challenging – don't take the medium of paint for granted!

Chapter twelve

In the primary school there can be an assumption that all painting media have similar properties and thus it is often an activity that is given a lower priority in staff development activities than other media and processes. In fact there is now a bewildering range of paint media available from educational suppliers for the teacher, so an understanding of their various properties is essential if they are to be used effectively. Although many pupils will paint without inhibition in the pre-school years, it is wrong to assume that this free approach will be maintained without teacher intervention as pupils progress. Their skills will only develop effectively if the teacher introduces painting tools and media systematically and encourages pupils to experiment, providing learning tasks that are challenging. This chapter will explore what the subject leader needs to know about what can sometimes be a neglected medium.

The medium of paint

Paints have varying properties and pupils should be given experience of a wide range, though they should not be introduced to too many at once as this might confuse them. The wise subject leader will want to choose one staple paint medium that will be used consistently throughout the school, so that pupils can gain confidence in its use. In the past the chosen medium was usually powder paint and this remains a popular choice because as a dry powder it requires pupils to mix

and discover a wide range of differing colours. It can be both mixed thinly and used as a thick impasto although, in fact, when used thinly often it can produce rather anaemic colour. For such thin transparent paint application, where the tones are lightened by allowing the white colour of the paper to show through, traditional solid watercolour paints are more effective. Even so powder colour has much to commend it, though it is now less used in the secondary school than the primary sector.

Occasionally pupils may enjoy working with solid blocks of poster colour, but these are too limited to be used as the prime source of paint in the classroom. Poster colours are useful where flat even colour effects are required. Poster colours also can be purchased in tubes although this would be too expensive to be the main paint medium for use throughout the school.

When colour mixing is not being prioritised the many ready-mixed paints that are now on the market are an easy to use alternative to powder colour. However it is worth pointing out that many of these liquid paints may comprise only basic powder colour mixed with water which, when their cost is considered, might make them seem an expensive convenience. Even when using liquid colours it is still important to encourage colour mixing – to always provide a separate brush in each differing colour container is to deny pupils a learning opportunity.

Whereas powder paint and other basic ready-mixed colours have a washable glue binder, acrylic paint, though also water-based, has a binder of plastic emulsion which will dry permanently with a sheen, rather than the matt surface of ordinary watercolours. Again it can be expensive to purchase for whole class use, and as it is essentially a mixture of a transparent acrylic base such as PVA glue and powder colour it is possible to get pupils to mix their own acrylic paints more cheaply. This will enable very thick colours to be mixed which can be applied by a palette knife. Oil colours are expensive and take a long time to dry and because they are not diluted with water are impractical for use in the primary school.

If children have developed a mastery of the use of basic powder colour, transparent watercolour, and acrylic paint, and can exploit the differing properties of each medium by the time they reach Year 6 they will be well prepared to paint with confidence in the secondary school. The subject leader should list the key learning activities for each year group in the school curriculum plan in order to achieve this goal.

Tools and techniques for painting

Obviously the most conventional way of applying paint is with a brush. A range of good brushes of different sizes is essential if pupils are to be able to master the processes of painting. Differing media require different brushes. Watercolour can be best applied using soft flexible brushes, while powder paint requires a harder

bristle. Brushes come in all sizes and shapes and pupil should have the chance to choose the most appropriate brush for the task in hand. A brush with a square end will produce a different effect from a round one; a fine brush will be needed for a delicate work, as in imitating the technique of the pointillists, and a much larger one is needed for bold gestural mark-making in the style of abstract expressionism. In order to gain control of the use of such a range of brushes it is important to encourage pupils to experiment with their differing effects, recording the range of outcomes in their sketchbooks for future reference. Focus this experimentation by giving them a range of words such as thin, heavy, hard and hairy and asking them to make a range of marks which best illustrates each word and then challenge their classmates to match the words to the painted outcomes.

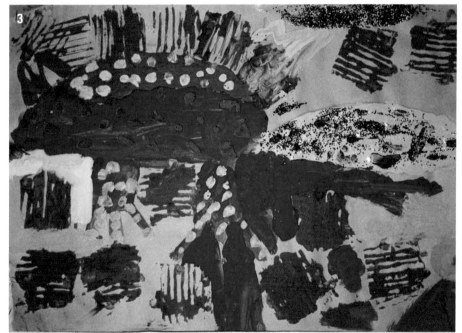

The range of effects that can be produced with a brush may be considerable but paint can be applied with almost anything, and as well as palette knives and pieces of card, interesting effects can be gained by applying paint with sponges or rag, by stippling with a stencil brush, flicking paint onto the surface using a toothbrush or even dribbling it from a stick. Pupils will relish the opportunity to experiment; paint thin layers of transparent paint in a series of thin glazes onto tissue paper. Try mixing acrylic paint thickly with sand to create textured surfaces, scratch through one painted layer to reveal a different colour underneath, drag thick paint over a

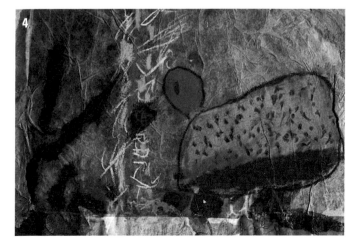

previously textured painted surface leaving some of the under painting exposed and do not neglect the possibilities of wax resist. It might even be possible to design a machine that paints! The aim of this experimental activity will be to develop an increasing understanding of media properties, the potential of tools and the many methods of application, which subsequently can be used for observational and expressive means. If pupils progressively increase their skill in controlling paint, the frustration that can be engendered as they become more critical of their work will be obviated.

Paint will usually be applied to paper. Good quality cartridge is essential if the paint is to adhere satisfactorily to the surface and the paper to remain reasonably flat after drying. Newsprint and cheap sugar papers are unsatisfactory substitutes that should be avoided. For watercolour heavier,

special textured papers may be introduced, though these are expensive. Painting onto dampened paper is particularly effective if using these papers. Stiffer card is needed if thick textured paint is to be applied effectively with a palette knife to a rigid surface. Though acrylic paint can be applied to almost any surface without preparation, very absorbent surfaces such as a brick wall for a mural may benefit from priming before application of the paint. If non-acrylic water-based colours, including powder paint, seem disappointingly flat and dull after drying the colour may be revitalised by being coating with very thin PVA, polyurethane varnish or even by buffing the surface to a sheen with a soft cloth after spraying with furniture polish.

All pupils occasionally should have the opportunity of working on an easel as opposed to the horizontal surface of a

table in order to discover how thick paint has to be mixed in order to stop it running – this is particularly important for pupils in the early years.

What colours to provide
The range of colours that should be provided should not always be so wide that it will discourage colour mixing. A basic set of the primaries can be supplemented with a green and a crimson red as well as vermilion and this will generate a wide range of subtle and close toned colours. Some colours however, such as an intense purple, are difficult to achieve by basic mixing and so this limited palette can be varied once in a while by including a wider range when the task demands it. For example, the use of fluorescent colours if complementary colours are being explored or contrasting red and green in the style of Bridget Riley's stripe paintings. A differing range

of colours will be also be produced if pupils are told to mix white with all the basic colours to explore pastel shades, or sometimes if black is removed so that pupils have to mix colours to get a more subtle range of very dark tones. However to always deny pupils the use of black or only ever allow the use of a very limited range of basic colours in order to ensure that the outcomes are always conventionally 'tasteful' is to restrict pupils' learning opportunities. Your objective is their confident selection of the most appropriate range of colours for the subject matter and the task in hand.

Exploring colour

The most obvious visual element that will be explored by using paint is colour, though the painting process involves mark making and the exploration of line and texture as well. The language of colour should be introduced systematically, with the curriculum plan outlining the key areas of knowledge about colour that are to be acquired at each stage, including when that knowledge is to be reinforced. For instance, pupils should understand that primary colours can be mixed to produce secondary colours and know what colours can be mixed to create tertiary colours, such as brown. They will develop a 'vocabulary' of colour by seeing how many different secondary colours they can mix from two basic primaries, and eventually know the difference between a tint and a shade. An understanding of the colour wheel is important though it can be taught without rigidly and painstakingly reproducing it; learning about colour can be developed through enjoying and exploring the medium of paint freely.

Staff development activity
Though I rarely visit a primary classroom where paint is not available it is less common to find that it is being used regularly, consistently and effectively. As subject leader you should consider staging a paint workshop for staff, providing the opportunity to experiment using the full range of paint media and tools. It can be linked with a colour activity thus exploring the medium and developing understanding of teaching the visual elements simultaneously. The pupils' confidence will grow as teacher expertise increases.

Don't take the medium of paint for granted!

Illustrations

1: Tools and media for painting

2-5: Using painting tools and media inventively

6: Designing a machine that paints

7-8: Control and subtlety in the use of paint will develop as pupils progress

9: Exploring shape and colour with paint

PRINTMAKING

Chapter thirteen

While it is sometimes neglected in the primary school, printmaking is an exciting way to explore imagery focusing particularly on the visual elements of texture and pattern. A printed image has a unique quality and records surface detail very accurately, in a manner that cannot be achieved in any other way. It is particularly helpful when exploring the visual element of texture.

Organisation and materials

There are a number of factors that inhibit printmaking with pupils, but the main one is the difficulty of organisation, given the large size of some primary classes and the problems generated by a potentially messy process. However it can be introduced effectively as a smaller group activity rather than a procedure that involves a whole class. Whatever the group size, to minimise problems it is essential to ensure that all working surfaces are covered in newspaper and that pupils are wearing overalls.

It is preferable to have a limited number of 'inking stations' in use in the class, with perhaps only two alternative colours available initially. Only water-based printmaking ink should be used, and though simple printmaking can take place using powder or ready-mixed paint these dry too quickly to be effective for block work or mono printing methods. You are advised to buy the correct medium from an educational supplier for the more complex processes. Adequate numbers of rubber rollers of differing widths are required, rigid

plastic laminate sheets to roll out the ink, and plenty of rags and sponges to clear up afterwards. The choice of paper can have considerable influence on the quality of a print. Thin paper including newsprint or coloured tissue that is flexible will often produce a better print than stiff paper with a strong texture if a press is not being used. This is all that is required for simple printmaking to take place.

Processes

Most skills in printmaking are acquired during engagement with the process, though pupils need to be shown how to roll out ink evenly onto a flat surface, and to use only the minimum amount of the medium that is needed. Commercially produced ink will be perfect for use straight from the tin or tube, but if ready mixed paint is being used it can take time to get the consistency just right. Pupils will also soon discover that it is usually best to lay the paper on top of a block that has been made and rub to make an effective print, rather than put the block onto the paper and apply pressure.

All of the printmaking processes I use in primary schools are simple and none require the use of a printing press. Many are suitable for working with Key Stage 1 pupils, but if you are inexperienced you are advised to have a go yourself before attempting to print with a class. A good starting point is to explore the concept that one can 'take a print from anything'. This will engage pupils in the process of visual inquiry by challenging them to print

from organic forms such as leaves or a sliced cabbage, differing flat wood grained planks, or any manufactured surfaces that are flat such as fabric or the soles of shoes. This is a logical extension of taking a rubbing from a surface, to reveal its texture and pattern. For these activities the ink or paint can be simply applied with a brush or sponge as effectively as using a roller.

It is possible to get interesting prints from the most unlikely sources; consider for instance printing from items of clothing such as an old shirt or shorts. This can be done most easily by making a sandwich of two sheets of hardboard and several sheets of paper laid on either side of the flattened out item of clothing after soaking it in thinned ready mixed paint. It may take a few attempts to get exactly the right amount of colour on the garment but very interesting outcomes can be produced. All of this activity extends pupils' perception of surface texture and will complement their observational work.

As well as printing a single impression of a found object, young pupils can combine prints from cotton reels, pieces of Lego and any other available bits and pieces, making complicated pictures or patterns to develop compositional skills. They should also be encouraged to enrich other work such as their paintings by printing onto them with these found objects, or re-using the outcomes of, for instance, a potato printing activity in a subsequent collage. Even printing from found objects is more meaningful if treated as a part of

...printmaking is an exciting way to explore imagery.

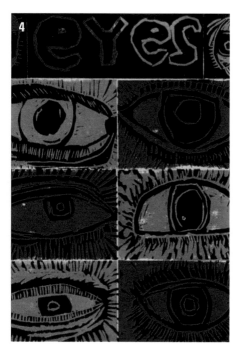

a continuous expressive project that enhances visual learning.

These improvised printmaking processes can become more structured with older pupils by building up relief printing blocks, gluing string, sandpaper and other flat surfaced found objects on a piece of hardboard. This is known as relief printing because the raised surface that is produced is inked up and can be printed without a press by laying paper over it and rubbing vigorously. Rather than solely relying on found objects, complex shapes can be cut out of card and glued onto the surface according to a pre-planned design which can then be used to explore principles of repeat patterning.

The alternative to printing where the raised surface is printed, is to cut into a flat surface so that the sections that are incised do not print. The simplest and most manageable medium for this is the sheets of fine polystyrene that are now available from art suppliers. These can be incised with almost anything including a pencil, or objects such pressed into the surface to create a pattern. The sheet is simply inked up after this procedure and the print is made. Lino may be a favoured alternative for older pupils but this is rather an intractable medium, though less resistant to cutting if warmed prior to being incised with a specialist tool. The lino should never be held by the hand during cutting,

as these very sharp tools can cut pupils if they slip, but rather braced against a vertical surface or ideally a bench hook utilised for support. Children should be very carefully supervised throughout the process for reasons of safety.

Stencil methods are another form of printmaking, and activities can vary from rolling ink across simple cut paper stencils to elementary versions of screen-printing. The latter involves squeezing ink through a silk mesh stretched over a simple frame, with a paper stencil underneath used to mask certain sections of the paper from the ink. This is best treated as a small group activity for older pupils. Art suppliers now provide a basic kit for such processes, which make them more manageable; it is essential to try this process out yourself before introducing it to pupils.

Of all simple primary print processes, mono printing is often the most flexible and exciting. The most basic method involves painting an image on any flat non-porous surface and taking a print from it. Only one (mono) print can be taken. Alternatively the complete surface can be rolled out with printing ink, with some sections subsequently removed using the finger, the end of a paintbrush or a rag before taking a print. This elementary process works well even for young pupils. Another method, to be introduced as pupils confidence

and control increases, involves rolling a very thin even film of ink onto a clean flat surface, that is left unmarked before the printing paper is dropped lightly on to it. Do not rub this but rather draw on the back of the paper. The pressure created by this means that it will pick up every fine detail of the drawing, and the paper can then be moved to a different colour surface and the process repeated to produce multi-coloured linear images that have a character similar to an etching. To produce a successful print it is essential to ensure that there is only a fine film of printing ink on the surface.

As subject leader you should encourage other staff to use printing as a part of a continuous process of visual enquiry rather than a way of only quickly producing slick and superficial end products. Dashing off a few surface prints before changing to another activity will not exploit its potential properly. Combining printmaking with other two-dimensional processes, by printing onto a pre-painted surface to enrich it will further sustain printmaking activities. The imagery that is being explored should be also carefully considered, with every opportunity being taken to enhance pupil powers of observation, and develop their understanding of the visual elements of pattern and texture. Printmaking has much to offer if it is planned carefully, presented progressively and given similar priority to other artistic processes.

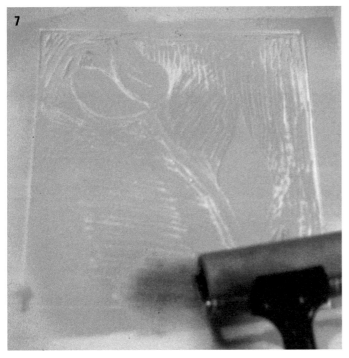

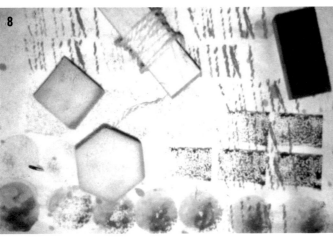

Illustrations

1-8: The illustrations show a range of differing printing processes using potato, found objects, lino, polystyrene and mono printing.

You can find detailed health and safety information pertinent to art and design in schools by accessing:

www.nsead.org/hsg/index.asp

CLAY WORK

Chapter fourteen

Many observers have noted that three-dimensional work in the primary school is an underdeveloped activity, with some pupils having little or no experience in this area apart from that which arises from design and technology. But three-dimensional work is an essential part of any curriculum planned by an art and design subject leader.

You will recall that in the chapter on curriculum planning, the 'processes and media' three-dimensional section was divided into modelling and constructing.

Modelling involves the manipulation of a plastic medium and constructing involves building using more rigid materials. Clay is the most important modelling medium in schools. As it can also be used for construction activities using coils or slabs and even carved in its 'leather hard' state, it is indeed a ubiquitous material, which should feature as a regular component in every pupil's balanced art and design education. Sadly it is less used now than in the past. It can be regarded as a messy material, not easily used in a classroom largely dominated by 'academic' concerns, and one that is difficult to organise. However some simple procedures can make clay more manageable for even a class of very young children and as subject leader you should encourage its use in every primary classroom.

Exploiting the full potential of clay

I have chosen the term 'clay work' carefully in this chapter for although clay has traditionally been used to make pots its properties are best exploited if it is regarded as a sculptural medium, which can be used in a range of ways for making many different three-dimensional objects. Almost anything that is produced in two dimensions can also be reproduced in three dimensions using clay.

It is important that pupils develop an understanding of the properties of clay. While from an early age they should be given every opportunity to enjoy and explore the medium for its own sake, they also need to know that the longer they manipulate a piece of clay the drier and more inflexible it becomes. It is important too that they know its origin and that it has a special magic in changing its nature when exposed to high temperature.

Pupils should develop these basic skills:

- How to join pieces of clay together using liquidised clay (slip) so that when the model/construction dries out pieces do not fall off.
- How to roll a coil that has an even cross section, using their hands.
- How to use a rolling pin balanced on wooden guides (which ensure consistency of thickness in the same way that pastry can be rolled out) to produce a slab of clay that can be used for construction.
- How to hollow out a solid piece of clay in such a way to avoid it exploding during firing.

Standards and functions

The same standard of work should be expected from clay activities that is demanded from pupils engaged in drawing or painting. They should be encouraged to revisit their work rather than always finish it in one session, add careful detail using tools and equipment appropriately, and exploit its the textural potential. At times they may design in advance for clay-work projects but working directly into the medium to explore ideas physically is equally important.

Clay can be used for the purposes of observation and recording (e.g. natural objects that have been drawn such as seed pods or objects such as shoes can be made in clay). It can be used imaginatively and expressively, (e.g. imaginary machines or dragons – see illustrations). It offers a range of possible critical studies links (e.g. introduce well-known sculptors and studio potters as sources of stimulus), and provides an opportunity to investigate the visual elements (e.g. interlocking spheres and hollows for form, or exploring texture and patterns in tile-making). Children will enjoy problem-solving team games with clay – challenging pupils to build the highest tower or roll the longest coil from a given amount of clay will generate intense competition. And of course they will

Clay is the most important modelling medium in schools.

enjoy making functional pots using rolled coils or constructed from slabs. Clay's potential is enormous and the buzz of excitement when children hear that clay is to be used is a reward in itself.

To fire or not to fire
One of the reasons that clay work is underdeveloped in schools is that teachers feel it is essential to fire clay to produce a finished product and a kiln may not always be available. The provision of a kiln is certainly very useful, though the time it takes to fire work can be an onerous task that is likely to fall on the shoulders of the subject leader. The location of a kiln is

important, for current safety regulations require that it to be in a separate, lockable area that is fireproof, away from pupils and with the fumes from the kiln extracted to the open air. If undaunted by this, a typical small kiln suitable for a primary school that works from a 13-amp socket will cost about £500 including installation, and to avoid being fired excessively the internal chamber dimensions need to be at least two cubic feet. However it is important to avoid buying a kiln that is so large that a special three–phase power supply is required. Professional advice should be sought before buying the kiln, for all these reasons.

Other methods of firing clay such as in a bonfire or using sawdust packed tightly in a bin are too difficult to manage safely and an ordinary domestic oven will not reach the required temperature. Clay will only change from its 'green' fragile dry state into the robust ceramic material we are all familiar with at a minimum temperature of about 800 degrees centigrade. The first (biscuit) firing should be done slowly after the work has been thoroughly dried. If clay is to be glazed it needs to be fired for a second time to over 1000 degrees centigrade after having been dipped into the liquid solution of the glaze. It needs to be emphasised that, as the glaze will melt during firing, the kiln needs to be packed carefully to avoid any of the objects being in contact, and there should be no glaze on the base of any of them. Because of the need to avoid contact during a glaze firing one biscuit firing produces at least three glaze firings. Many subject leaders may decide that leaving the biscuit ware unglazed is the most sensible solution. If glazing is to be attempted, start simply by buying ready-mixed coloured glazes from a recognised stockist and experimenting with these before attempting to mix your own.

All is not lost if a school does not have a kiln, for allowing clay sculpture to dry completely and then carefully painting it and varnishing with a polyurethane varnish can actually produce quite a solid and reasonably permanent model.

The coloured finish is actually more controllable than with glazing, the scale of work can be much larger than that which is constrained by the size of the kiln and solid models do not have to be hollowed out to avoid explosion during firing. It is possible also to buy clay that has an additive that hardens without firing. Possession of a kiln is not essential and should not inhibit schools from using clay.

Organising the use of clay in school
There is little merit in the practice of ordering clay bodies in different colours. Choose standard earthenware clay. It will be delivered in plastic bags, which will preserve the clay at a workable consistency until it is opened. As soon as clay is exposed to the air, and to the willing but warm hands of pupils, it will start to dry out. After being used by pupils any surplus clay that remains malleable can be put back into the bag with a very small amount of water being added and then tied up so that is completely airtight to be used again. On-going work will remain moist if wrapped and sealed in a plastic bag. A few plastic dustbins are the obvious place to keep the clay when not in use, but if space is at a premium it can be stored in an outside storeroom – a matter for negotiation with your caretaker.

Reconstituting clay that has dried out is a laborious and messy process; unfired dried clay needs to be immersed completely into water and, after absorbing the water, dried on a plastic slab in the open before wedging. I do not think it is worth the considerable effort involved. Obviously clay that has been fired cannot be reconstituted.

Among so many art processes that you are likely to use with children clay work is potentially the messiest. Wooden boards are an essential work surface, as clay will stick onto any non-absorbent surface, so do not work directly on plastic tables. However the board should be large enough to facilitate large-scale work when appropriate. MDF board cut into 60 centimetre square pieces is one possibility.

Most tools for clay use can be improvised. Blunt kitchen knives will supplement conventional clay tools made ideally from hardwood or plastic. Wire clay loops, for gouging coils from clay can be made easily and a range of interesting objects is helpful to make patterns in clay. Rolling pins and wooden guides to ensure that the slabs that are rolled are consistent in thickness are probably the only other tools that are needed. Clay use in the primary school can be agreeably low on technological requirements.

Clay dust is a health hazard though good housekeeping will obviate problems. The boards and all working surfaces together with tools should be cleaned at the end of every activity to avoid unnecessary dust being generated from dried clay. Any dried clay that is not being fired or painted should not be left exposed in the teaching environment. Children should of course wear aprons and these should be washed regularly; this is definitely a case for an adult relative's discarded shirt!

Staff development activity

The training days I most enjoy when working with teachers are those when we use clay. It is a medium that even the most inhibited staff member will enjoy and can use successfully and so the subject leader who is charged with expanding staff in-service opportunities can raise the status of the subject in an unthreatening way. Try starting the work by blindfolding the teachers and asking them to make a simple figure in five minutes from a lump of clay. Many will produce a figure that is recognisable as clay is first and foremost a tactile material. The laughter that is always generated in the group will be an excellent icebreaker to start the day. Then divide into groups and see who can build the highest tower from a standard lump of clay – the competition will be fierce. With three-dimensional work declining as a primary art and design activity, clay is a good place to start your staff-training programme aimed at raising the profile of the subject.

Illustrations

1-5: Examples of free modelling and construction work using clay

3D WORK

Chapter fifteen

The limited amount of three-dimensional work taking place in primary schools has been noted in the previous chapter on clay. The reasons for this are complex but some staff simply do not believe the activity is important enough to risk the problems of organisation and management. Making a case for three-dimensional work is an important task for you as subject leader. With a chapter of this handbook already devoted to three-dimensional modelling work in clay, this final section will be concerned exclusively with three-dimensional construction activities. A distinction has already been made in the previous chapter between modelling (manipulating a flexible plastic medium, usually clay) and constructing (using resistant materials to build sculptural outcomes). When clay is cut into slabs and joined with a slip this is also a form of construction but there are many other materials that can be used.

The case for three-dimensional work

To generate confidence encourage staff to recognise that starting points for three-dimensional work can be exactly the same as those for two-dimensional activity; if a pupil can draw or paint something, be it observed or imagined, they can and should also be able to make it. Explain that the important visual element of 'form' can only be explored and understood through three-dimensional activity, and a rounded critical studies programme must include references to sculptors and sculpture.

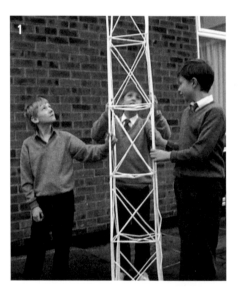

Also remind staff that there are pupils who find three-dimensional work less exacting, as it does not involve the reduction of three dimensions into two, which can be a challenge to which some boys in particular may not respond. Indeed it may be that little or no preparatory two-dimensional design work needs to take place in advance of the actual physical process of making, catering particularly to the kinaesthetic type of learner. One only has to watch how naturally children play with construction toys, or even as adults build structures from trees and stones found in the environment, to realise how compulsive is the desire to construct.

Managing three-dimensional activities

Even if staff do recognise the importance of three-dimensional work, my research suggests that the problems encountered in organising and managing materials and supervising the processes, coupled with a lack of knowledge of sculptural processes are the major constraints. With class sizes in primary schools now averaging thirty it is inevitable that complex practical activities will pose particular organisational problems, though not all three-dimensional materials are potentially messy. The solutions depend on the school context, but if space is a constraint identified in the audit, subject leaders should consider reducing the scale of three-dimensional work, or alternatively plan three-dimensional as a smaller group activity, possibly 'sub-managed' by the classroom assistant. The ideal would be to offer such experiences in a dedicated

One only has to watch how naturally children play with construction toys, or even as adults, build structures from trees and stones found in the environment, to realise how compulsive is the desire to construct.

4

5

3

area, equipped with tools, materials and workbenches if there is the luxury of a vacant area in the school that can be claimed for this purpose. A final possibility, though certainly not ideal, is to concentrate the yearly 'art week' on a whole school three-dimensional project, which might even spread out into other open spaces in the school and the playground. However to merely engage in three-dimensional work for one week in a year hardly meets the requirements of continuity and progression outlined in a previous chapter. Problems of long term storage can be obviated if pupils are encouraged to record the outcomes of their three-dimensional activities for assessment purposes on a CD before taking it home.

Simple starting points

Encourage your less confident colleagues to start simply by collecting and using improvised materials for construction work to make junk sculpture. Cardboard boxes, lolly sticks, tin cans, egg boxes, discarded mechanical bits-and-pieces and organic found objects such as fir cones can all be joined together to construct robots and creatures of all shapes and sizes. The youngest pupils can use Sellotape, paperclips, sticky tape and elastic bands for joining pieces together. A paper stapler will make a more permanent join, pieces can be bound together quite securely using soft binding wire for metal, or bonded with impact adhesive or glue guns for card or balsa wood. Given such simple provision, pupils will improvise readily and enthusiastically to make exciting pieces.

In the primary school, where subject boundaries are not clearly defined, it is difficult to decide exactly where art and design ends and technology begins, so problem-solving activities with three-dimensional materials offer another interesting starting point at the interface of the disciplines. Setting small scale problems, such as a competition to see who can build the highest tower using art straws, designing simple jewellery that moves, or a hat that can be worn by two pupils, or large-scale challenges such as building a raft, will require pupils to use materials inventively and produce ingenious solutions without the need for significant teacher intervention.

At the same time it is desirable to introduce pupils to some more formal construction processes, particularly with the older children. Starting simply, stockings can be stuffed with newspaper to commence constructing snakelike creatures. Or bind willow withies (normally used for basket making) and clad them with tissue coated with PVA. Perhaps make helmets for costumes by coating the face (protected by tissue – try it yourself first!) with brown sticky tape and even use ordinary newspaper rolled tightly into long thin spills which are surprisingly rigid.

As a more complex alternative, screwed up newspaper, card or soft wire can form an armature, which is then clad using 'Modroc', a fabric bandage impregnated with dried powdered Plaster of Paris, once widely used for making plaster casts in hospitals. It can be cut into manageable pieces with a pair of scissors, dipped into a saucer of water without entirely saturating the fabric and then wrapped round the armature, where it will rapidly dry to produce a rigid sculptural form. This can be a messy process that needs to be carefully supervised, particularly with young children, but the outcomes can be very impressive, particularly when painted with acrylic paint to give additional colour, rigidity and protection. An introductory session with staff on an CPD training day using Modroc is desirable, led either by the confident subject leader, or an external consultant who understands the process, before it is adopted extensively across school.

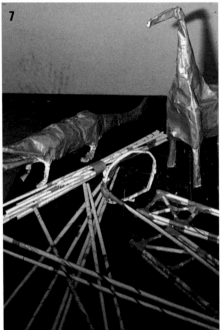

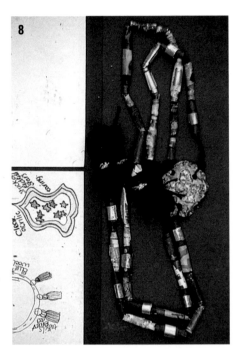

These are just some of the three-dimensional processes that are available for use in the primary school but it is beyond the scope of this handbook to expand further, though a scrutiny of the materials and processes utilised in the illustrations may provide more ideas. However it is important not to fall into the trap of suggesting to staff that three-dimensional work is difficult and requires much special knowledge, as they could use this as a reason not to do it. Until confidence develops the subject leader should encourage the use of simple materials, with improvisation and experimentation at the centre.

Tools and safe practice

Similarly the tools that are needed for three-dimensional activities are probably all readily available in schools as a result of the introduction of design and technology. All classrooms should now have a basic set of hammers, pliers, simple saws, cutting knives and simple safe power tools and so on, which can be called in to use for sculptural artistic processes as well as technology activities. When coupled with glue guns, highly complex structures can be made using very simple methods. Pupils obviously should be encouraged to use such tools at a permanent workstation with a bench and a vice. Safe practice with all equipment is of paramount importance and if there is any doubt children should be supervised closely during their use and wear appropriate protective gear. The appendix of the subject documentation provided by the subject leader must include advice on Health and Safety procedures.

Extensive information on safe practice in art and design education can be found on the NSEAD web site at **www.nsead.org/hsg/index.aspx**

Three-dimensional environments

Without regular and progressive opportunities to work in three dimensions the primary pupil will not receive a broad and balanced art and design education. What is most likely is that the subject leader will have to convince hard pressed, non-specialist staff that this is an essential part of pupils' creative art and design experience if it is to feature in every year group. The best way forward is to demonstrate by example, particularly if the outcomes spread outside the classroom and into more public spaces, which is why I have often built elaborate jungles in corridors and entrance halls, with trees made from cardboard tubes, branches from twisted paper and multicoloured leaves and fronds, all suspended from the ceiling or even built sculpture from snow in the school grounds. The enthusiasm with which pupils engage in such activities, the sense of wonder generated when others view the results and the overall impact on the environment will encourage others to introduce three-dimensional work to their pupils.

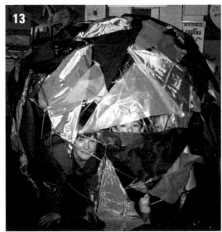

Illustrations

1: Problem solving with straws

2-3: Building with scrap material

4: Casting in plaster

5: Building with scrap material

6: Sculpture using 'mod-roc'

7: Paper spills rolled to make animals

8: Jewellery from sweet papers

9: Building with boxes

10: Snow sculpture based on Henry Moore

11: Found object sculpture by the author

12: Stocking 'snakes'

13: Withies and tissue – a 3D version of a
      Georgia O'Keefe picture

I hope this book has developed your thinking about your role as the subject leader in art and design in your school. Not everything you have read will be relevant. How you approach the responsibilities will depend on the context in which you work. However by systematically following the strategies I have described many subject leaders tell me they have established art and design as a significant curriculum experience in the education of primary pupils. Given that so many pupils in secondary schools cease their art studies after only three years it is essential to maximise the opportunities for visual creative activities in the earlier years.

Good luck in your endeavours.

John Bowden

FURTHER INFORMATION

The National Society for Education in Art and Design is the leading national authority concerned with art, craft and design across all phases of education in the United Kingdom. We offer, for a single subscription, the extensive benefits of membership of a professional association, a learned society and the option of membership of an independent trade union.

The NSEAD provides:

- Immediate access to information to keep you up to date with news, views and current developments in art and design education
- Opportunities to participate in debates about art and design and wider educational issues and to make contact with collegues from all phases of education accross the UK and worldwide
- Recognition by government and governmental agencies – the society is consulted regularly and advises on issues related to the subject and more general matters

- Frequent professional development opportunites through an extensive programme of international, national and regional events
- Publications including newsletters and 3 issues of the International Journal of Art & Design Education each year and the option of subscribing to START magazine for those working in a primary phase
- Access to the NSEAD online mail order specialist book shop
- Efficient professional advice on all aspects of employment in education: legal aid is also available if necessary
- Independence – the NSEAD is not affiliated to any other union or political party
- Insurance cover against theft of personal effects at work

CONTACT US

NSEAD
The Gatehouse
Corsham Court
Corsham
Wiltshire
SN13 0BZ

T. 01249 714825
F. 01249 716138

www.nsead.org